BY LOCK & POUND

BY LOCK
& POUND

by

Vivian Bird

B

M & M BALDWIN
Cleobury Mortimer, Salop
1988

This book is dedicated to

ROBERT ('BOB') LEVELL

tough walker and splendid listener
over many hundreds of miles
across the hills and on the level

Published by M & M Baldwin, 24 High Street,
Cleobury Mortimer, Kidderminster, Worcs DY14 8BY

Typesetting by Action Typesetting Ltd, Imperial House,
Russell St, Gloucester GL1 1NE

Printed by Billing & Sons Ltd, Hylton Rd,
Worcester WR2 5JU

Cover designed by Jeremy Mallard

Contents

Illustrations

Maps

Publisher's Foreword

When the author made the trips described in this book, few people realised how quickly and completely commercial traffic would disappear from Britain's smaller canals. This book is, therefore, particularly valuable as a record of actual working practice and conditions aboard a variety of cargo-carrying craft nearly 40 years ago. To his undoubted skills as a writer, Vivian Bird adds the inquiring mind of the journalist, which makes his book not only a rewarding read, but also an excellent source of information about commercial boats and their world. Although there exist quite a number of published accounts of narrow boat trips, journeys on broader-beamed craft have been described far less frequently. It is, therefore, particularly pleasing to be able to present here two of the latter: from Cardiff to Worcester, and from Nottingham to Hull.

Because of the documentary nature of this book, it is worth recording the dates of the trips:

Chapter 1:   King's Norton to Tardebigge: October 1951
              Oldbury to Nechells: April 1952
Chapter 2:   BBC cruise around Birmingham: July 1952
Chapter 3:   Cardiff to Worcester: August 1952
              Worcester to Tardebigge: August 1967
Chapter 4:   Cobley to King's Norton: February 1953
              Lapworth to Stratford: Spring 1953
Chapter 5:   King's Norton to Paddington: May/June 1953
Chapter 6:   Oldbury to Ellesmere Port: August 1953
Chapter 7:   Birmingham to Hull: September 1953

Much has changed during the intervening thirty-five years, although all the routes travelled by the author may still be cruised today. For this reason, although the text stands as it was written, no attempt has been made to provide a modern commentary. In particular, pre-decimal prices have been left untouched, without the totally misleading 'conversions' which so often distort perceptions of older values. Suffice it to remind readers that there were, before 1971, twelve pence to the shilling, and twenty shillings to the pound. The reader must, however, keep in mind that the author's comments and perspectives are those of the early 1950s. At a few points, the opportunity has been taken to add footnotes to expand on the original text, but these have been kept to a minimum.

The photographs have all been provided by the author, with the exception of No. 11 (National Waterways Museum, Gloucester) and No. 24 (Waterways Museum, Stoke Bruerne). Nos. 22 and 26 first appeared in the *Birmingham Weekly Post*. We are grateful for permission to use these.

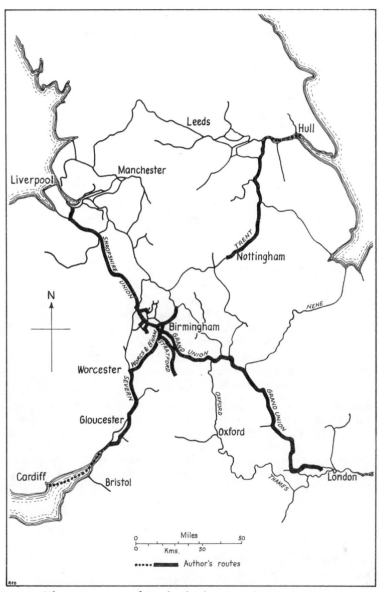

1: The waterways of England, showing the Author's cruises

INTRODUCTION

*In which an idea, begotten of canal tunnels, is
born beneath Snow Hill railway arch in darkest
Birmingham.*

From Snow Hill Station, Birmingham, I have travelled by trains
of the old Great Western Railway, south-east to Paddington,
south-west to Penzance, and north-west to Shrewsbury for
various destinations in Wales. So have countless thousands of
passengers. The one half-cardinal direction in which there is no
service direct from Snow Hill is north-east. Southbound trains run
out of the station through a tunnel to emerge at Moor Street.
Northward the elevated track lies over a succession of arches,
familiar to Birmingham people as they pass on their daily occasions
down Snow Hill and Livery Street.

The railway is an accepted method of transport; its metals well
travelled; its routes and termini well known. But of the thousands
who travel daily northward out of Snow Hill Station, how many
are aware that from a position almost immediately below the end
of the platforms, one could travel by water to the sea along all four
half-cardinal directions?

It was that fact which determined me to write this book,
dawning upon me suddenly as it did one April morning in 1952 as
I stood aboard Thomas Clayton's narrow boat TOWY beneath the
massive, but to many unsuspected, arch which carried the
northbound railway out of Snow Hill Station over the
Birmingham Canal. Despite the sweeping grace of the arch it is a
scene of gloom, but the light of inspiration dawns in unlikely
places.

I was travelling with TOWY from Oldbury to Nechells
Gasworks to write a story for my paper, the *Birmingham Weekly
Post.* By leaving our course and taking the next canal branch to the
right, just beyond the bridge at the junction of Corporation Street

9

and Aston Road, we could find our way through Bordesley, past Sampson Road wharf, to the Warwick & Birmingham Canal, and so to the Grand Union and London — still a fairly busy canal.

Back half-a-mile in our wake, up Farmer's Locks which convey the Birmingham Canal through the city, was a branch to the south, down which the canal could be seen burrowing beneath Broad Street, with the graceful spire of the Church of the Messiah rising above the short tunnel. There, in the basin beside Gas Street, is Worcester Bar where, for many years, a narrow 'bar' of brickwork divided the Birmingham Canal from the Worcester & Birmingham Canal, to prevent the latter — the newer company — drawing water from the former. Goods had then to be transhipped at the Bar, until differences were composed and the Bar severed.

A stop lock was then constructed to regulate the flow of water, and passing this TOWY could have taken me by canal to Worcester, thence down the Severn to the Gloucester & Berkeley Canal, and the tidal Severn at Sharpness — south-west by water to the sea. From Oldbury where our journey had begun in the early morning darkness, TOWY could — indeed often had — chugged her way to the Shropshire Union Canal and Ellesmere Port, three days distant on the Manchester Ship Canal and the Mersey.

So much for SE, SW, and NW. All these directions are fairly straightforward and in general use, though there is not much traffic on the Worcester & Birmingham Canal. North-east to the sea would be a trickier proposition. It scarcely seemed a feasible thing to send goods from Birmingham by water to the Humber. But the waterways are there if need be.

TOWY had moved on as I pondered my brainwave, and we were taking a sharp right turn on an aqueduct across the River Tame at Salford Bridge into the 'home straight' for the gasworks. To continue ahead instead of turning would have taken us into the Birmingham & Fazeley Canal, through Bromford and Tyburn out of the city, by-passing Tamworth on the northern section of the Coventry Canal, and eventually at Fradley Junction, on to the Trent & Mersey Canal. A turn through Burton and, at Derwent Mouth, we would breast the River Trent and follow its smug and silver length to the Humber.

I decided to travel these four waterways to the sea — to Severn, Mersey, Humber, and Thames, and as I made my first enquiries another interesting fact emerged. The Transport Act of 1947 had transferred 17 independently-owned waterway concerns, two State-owned, and 30 owned by the former railway companies to the British Transport Commission. They have practically all been unified under the Docks & Inland Waterways Executive. For convenience of management and control the D.I.W.E. has been broken down into four divisions, each relating to a major estuary and port area, and my plan would involve an incursion into the estuarial home waters of each area — North-Eastern based on the Humber, North-Western on the Mersey, South-Eastern on the Thames, and South-Western on the Severn. Thus was additional point and pattern given to my project.

But there is more to writing a book than its initial conception. An original theme is desirable, and this I felt I had. Then, the author lives with his work over a long period — it had better be pleasant. I felt sure canal-going would meet this requirement, though as yet I had done little. I had read with keen enjoyment Emma Smith's *Maidens' Trip* on the wartime experiences of girl boatmen plying the Grand Union between London and Birmingham, and had quickly jettisoned her second book on an Indian theme. I rated L.T.C.Rolt's *Green and Silver* among the best books on Ireland, though as a lover of Ireland not yet converted to a love of inland waterways I resented its library classification under the latter rather than the former heading.

I lived near the Warwick & Birmingham Canal at Acocks Green, and many of my articles had been written sitting beside it in the piquant resinous smell from Cartwright's timber yard across its waters. There I had watched and written about the conversion of ALBERT, a narrow boat, one of the earliest diesel-driven craft on the Grand Union, into DULCE DOMUM, the houseboat home of Peter Alun Jones and his bride Wendy. Champion sculler of Jesus College, Oxford, Mr Jones spent his 1951 long vacation making his home in time for his marriage after towing the boat, mainly by hand, across Birmingham from Tyburn to Acocks Green. In early October, complete with kitchen, living-room

furnished with antiques, single cabin, double cabin, study, bath-
room, hot and cold water, central heating and the usual offices,
DULCE DOMUM moved off to Oxford, there to house Mr and Mrs
Jones and a 'lodger' — Mr Jones's erstwhile college room-mate.
As a home DULCE DOMUM may have been economical; as a convey-
ance she wasn't, costing 9d. a mile in dues to the D.I.W.E.

Sitting beside the canal at Acocks Green I often passed the time
of day with boatmen bound for Tyseley Wharf, their boats and
butties low in the water with cargoes of metal ingots. The man
usually steered the boat; his wife the butty. Sometimes there was
a dog kennel aboard, and my children were delighted when once
they saw a hen squatting beside the gay Braunston bucket, an ever-
present feature of the complete narrow boat. Always the brass on
the chimney-stack shone brightly, colourful roses and castles
decorated the cabin door, while within glimpses could be had of
the traditional lace-edged plates hanging on the walls.

Tiring at times of writing, I had often walked the towpath
through Olton towards Solihull, a stretch of canal unfairly vilified
by E. Temple Thurston in his book named after his boat, *The
Flower Of Gloster*. My actual canal-going before TOWY had been
restricted to cruises between King's Norton and Tardebigge on the
Worcester & Birmingham Canal, aboard NORMAN CHAMBERLAIN,
the converted narrow boat belonging to the Birmingham
Federation of Boys' Clubs. NORMAN CHAMBERLAIN will glide into
these pages again, so more of her anon. Except that she —
confound people who will give masculine names to feminine boats
— did three things for me.

She was my introduction to Paul Winterforde-Young, ex
novice monk and miniature submariner, secretary of the Birmingham Federation, who conceived her and brought her into such
fruitful life. I was present at the launching OF NORMAN
CHAMBERLAIN on September 9th, 1951. The second boon she
bestowed upon me was the satisfaction of 'making something go'.
At 41 years I can't drive a car and have no wish to do so in the mad
juggernaut rush of the modern road. But on a canal one can 'drive'
without risk to oneself and others. To stand at the tiller of a canal
boat and, avoiding seen banks and unseen shoals, to take her

gently on her way at 4 m.p.h. is to know a rare peaceful satisfaction, whether it be through long straight stretches of Telford canal, or on the earlier winding waterways of Brindley.

Indeed, I take no little pride in some of my achievements at the tiller of NORMAN CHAMBERLAIN. Certainly I have run her aground on occasion. All her helmsman have. But when I recall some bends I have negotiated on the tortuous canal between King's Norton and Tardebigge — without slowing down — I feel no little elation. Knowing nought of anything mechanical, I did not know for many months how to use the gadgets which start her, stop her, slow her down, and put her in reverse. From someone ignorant of my ignorance I would take over the tiller and charge ahead at unreduced speed round bends where others would merely creep, and more often than not I came through unscathed.

The third and final experience for which I have to thank NORMAN CHAMBERLAIN is my introduction to canal tunnels. As a journalist I have travelled in many conveyances above, on, and below the ground, and had a wide variety of experience. None, however, approaches in interest and eerie excitement the passage of a canal tunnel when the weather is so dull that the other end cannot be seen. This is indeed to enter into the unknown. From the moment I first entered Wast Hill Tunnel beyond King's Norton aboard NORMAN CHAMBERLAIN I think this book was inevitable.

June 1953

CHAPTER ONE

*Tells of an October canal cruise through the
countryside and its peace, and of an April
passage through the city and its industry.*

Throughout Birmingham and the Black Country, lying forlorn in
canal arms and backwaters, are the skeletons and hulks of many old
narrow boats and butties whose usefulness in their heyday entitles
them to more honourable rest. Occasionally an impecunious but
ingenious home-builder purchases one of the better-preserved and
removes it for conversion into a floating residence. People come
from far afield in search of the derelict boats of the Black Country.
The epic is fresh in my mind of Dick Williams who, with some
help from his father and a pole, manhandled one such relic, which
cost him £50 at Dudley, down to Shalford, Surrey, taking 190
locks in his stride. When converted, this boat is intended as a
home for Mr Williams, a friend, and their brides.

An even nobler destiny awaited a waterlogged butty at
Oldbury. RUBY had lived one useful life carrying general cargo
between Birmingham and London, and later taking slack from
Cannock Collieries to Stourport Power Station. Then, her day
apparently done, she settled steadily on the bottom of an arm at
Oldbury. But like the ROYAL GEORGE of Cowper's poem 'her
timbers yet are sound and she may float again', and float again she
did when Paul Winterforde-Young had one of those flashes of
inspiration which make him an ideal leader of the young, to set up
a training boat for the Federation of Boys' Clubs in Birmingham.

Almost a year after the idea came the fulfilment. In October
1950 RUBY was taken over through the generosity of Mrs Enid
Schonegeval, who provided for the purchase and initial
conversion. Within the next eleven months some fifty firms
generously gave equipment — searchlight, twin horn electric
hooter, marine engine, mattresses — all that Paul's heart could

14

desire. A broadcast appeal for funds was made by the Chief Constable of Birmingham. Many willing helpers, boys from the clubs, their parents, and well-wishers gave their time and skill. And a proud and attractive craft was launched on the face of the waters at the Birmingham Small Arms sports ground on September 9th, 1951, by Mrs Schonegeval, and named NORMAN CHAMBERLAIN after her brother, killed as a captain in the Grenadier Guards during the First World War. He had been a keen worker for the less fortunate boys of Birmingham, and his spirit would accompany boys of a later generation on their cruises.

Paul's idea was that each week-end the boat should take fourteen boys and three volunteer adult staff on a cruise from the basin in King's Norton Factory Centre, down the Worcester & Birmingham Canal to Tardebigge. On a Sunday in October 1951 I first travelled over the ten miles of this lovely and exciting route with a dozen adult embryo helmsmen for NORMAN CHAMBERLAIN.

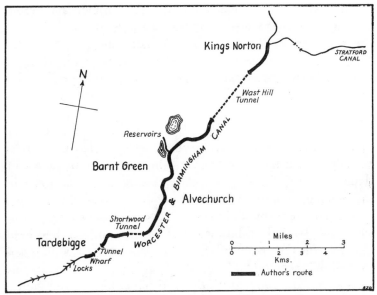

2: The Worcester & Birmingham Canal

After a day when all proved satisfactory, we emerged from Wast Hill Tunnel into a pea-soup fog on the last lap home. The engine was cut, and grovelling a laughing way along the towpath we bow-hauled the boat in, all feeling competent to take whatever might come when she started her new lease of life as a training craft the following week-end.

On this great occasion, the last week-end in October, when falling leaves carpeted the canal, accommodation aboard was limited and journalists as such superfluous. It was therefore as lecturer I joined the ship's company, the role to include assisting with the steering. It being the maiden training voyage and therefore experimental, adults were taking two of the boys' places. 'Captain of the Starboard Watch' was Ken Malin while, with 16 hearty trenchermen dependent upon him, Bob Flint was cook. Paul was, of course, skipper. Twelve boys sharing this pioneering venture paid 12 shillings each, and to see us off as NORMAN CHAMBERLAIN chugged carefully stern first from the basin to the canal was Mr Jack Mould, Chairman of the Federation.

The whistles from several football matches emphasised how differently we were spending our Saturday afternoon as NORMAN CHAMBERLAIN negotiated her first hazards — a 400 yards backwards crawl past the shoals alongside King's Norton Paper Mill, a turning manoeuvre at the junction with the Stratford Canal, the first place where this may be done, and a brush with a tug from Sharpness near the brickworks. Surmounting these difficulties, within half an hour of casting off we found ourselves gliding through a deepening bush-clad cutting towards the thrill of the journey, the Wast Hill Tunnel. A cold dank air met us as we approached the ornate portal. Our electric horn sounded a double note. "Searchlight on," shouted Paul through the megaphone from the tiller, and as we left daylight behind I focussed our beam on the brickwork two feet from our right-hand side, thus giving the helmsman one fixed point on which to steer. If that point becomes brighter the boat is moving too near that wall; if dimmer, too far from it.

We pressed steadily forward, the throb of the engine bringing some comfort in an eeriness at once repelling and fascinating.

Astern the bright circle of the entrance dwindled, but the pinpoint of light 2726 yards away at the other end remained distant and elusive. The outside world seemed far away. We were alone; an isolated community moving in a pool of our own radiance, lamplit patterns of the saloon windows on glistening walls, the illuminated archway beyond our bows reflected so faithfully in water still enough as to be invisible so that we appeared to be borne forward in mid-air along a cylinder of damp bricks.

Seated on the roof, linked by a stout rope, the boys experienced an initial period of awe and wonderment. Invisible fingers brushed their faces, the dangling ends of the broken telephone cable once used to facilitate traffic through the tunnel. Every mind was occupied with thoughts of what we should do if the chugging of the engine were to cease. But it continued reassuringly, and a song was raised to Clementine in regions more appropriate to Eurydice. At three points we passed beneath air shafts, slender openings with overhanging shrubs silhouetted against a far-off disc of sky. Little light but much water came down each shaft, to be rudely disturbed as our timbers thrust forward. Beyond the third shaft the exit enlarged rapidly until tendrils of ivy could be seen hanging from the outer brickwork. But we had to run the gauntlet of several showers dripping through the roof before we gained the outer world again. Wast Hill Tunnel, completed in 1797, is a wet tunnel.

We emerged into a cutting which for all its autumn tints seemed delightfully green after the gloom of our half hour underground. And so on through a chilly afternoon, the yellow autumn sun sending long shadows over ploughland pungent with manure. From the bridge at Hopwood, Mr Frank Chamberlain, Vice-Chairman of the Federation, waved a hail and farewell just before we settled down for tea. The top bunks, metal folding contraptions with mattresses attached, and suspended from the roof by chains, serve as tables, and there is ample arm-room.

The meal over, we sat on deck, three boys peeling potatoes, while the rest of us enjoyed the passing scene, ducking as low branches swept overhead. Lower Bittell Reservoir disappeared round a bend, a beautiful white house beside an aqueduct passed

astern, and across a field 200 yards away a procession of cars
hurried along the main Birmingham – Redditch road in noisy
contrast to our leisurely unfrequented waterway. As dusk fell, a
fisherman tipped back his afternoon's catch from a keep-net,
stowed his rods, and departed homeward.

I risked a prentice hand on the helm, not without success, until
becoming involved with an overhanging alder I realised why
boatmen are notorious for their picturesque language. From the
bows the searchlight picked out the banks in russet and green. The
plop of a water rat, the rustle of a bird disturbed on a bough, were
the only sounds in the stillness, but for a boy dangling his legs
down the forepeak hatch who remarked "I like this, it's
peaceful."

At 7.30 p.m. we tied up at Shortwood, our night's mooring
deep in the country, and did justice to Bob's repast of boiled cod
with parsley sauce, peas, carrots, and potatoes, followed by stewed
apples, custard, and coffee. Then, with the bunks fixed sofa
fashion, sitting on the lower ones while using the upper ones
folded as backrests, we had a lecture and discussion session dealing
mainly with the history of canals, aided by the weather which beat
a steady tattoo of rain on the cabin roof, taking young minds off
exciting prospects of prowling in the surrounding woods. Later
we did some bushranging while the Plough hung low over
Birmingham and the glow from our windows was barely seen on
the grass of the moonlit clearing among the waterside trees. We
turned in with three blankets and a sleeping bag each. Through
the night came the laboured puffing of a train ascending the Lickey
Incline three miles away — and sleep.

Whatever rain the darkness had brought had washed every
cloud out of the sky next morning as Paul, standing on the deck,
led a short service before breakfast. Behind him a scrubland of
willow-herb and tangled shrubs rose from the far bank to a
brilliant sky. He had scarcely read from Saint Matthew 6-26:
'Behold the birds of the air', when, in a flash of salmon pink and
shining blue, a kingfisher skimmed past to disappear in the cutting
where sunlit silver birches stood gracefully above alders still dark
in the shadows.

After breakfast we cast off and cleared Shortwood Tunnel (613 yards) to a reach where anglers were preparing for a Sabbath Day's meditation, beating out places among the nettles, one with a keep-net big enough to secure the Loch Ness monster, another greasing his line. The boys serenaded these enthusiasts with 'The Fisher-men of England' and a running fire of badinage leapt between barge and bank. Paul, plying the tiller with one hand and with the other scanning distant horizons through a telescope, was variously likened to Nelson and Captain Hornblower. On a bend beneath a huge orchard our most desperate attempts failed to keep NORMAN CHAMBERLAIN off a mudbank. With a breaking of branches and a scraping from our keel we hit the shore, causing a contemplative figure to fall backwards off his fishing basket.

By deploying our combined weight advantageously, and with some shoving on a pole, we got under way again and I took over the tiller for Tardebigge Tunnel (580 yards), which has little brickwork, being cut mainly in solid rock. We made the passage without detriment to boat or tunnel, and tied up along Tardebigge Wharf below the garish church spire.

Mr J.C. Beckett was kind enough to show us over the 500 acres of his Hewell and Brockhill Farms, where he produces 260 gallons of milk daily from about 260 Friesians and Guernseys, introducing us to 'Model Roma', a Friesian who has given more than 50 tons of milk in her nine years, and amazing us with a demonstration of the cleanly habits of his pigs.

Replete with tomato soup, roast beef, cabbage, potatoes, stewed apple, rice pudding, and cheese we re-entered Tardebigge Tunnel at 2.15 p.m. under stormy skies, and as our bows reached the northern end there came a shout "Take her back in, it's pouring out here". Our passage home was excellent. Seeking deep water on the bend which proved our undoing on our outward journey, we swept among the overhanging willows, and I managed to clutch the tiller with one hand, hold on my hat and guard my face with the other, and yet keep us off the bottom. At one point we ran beneath a crab tree and half stripped it. For tea we stopped above Bittell Reservoir and saw an exquisite sunset. The water was in turn flame, pink, purple, and slate-coloured with the Lickey Hills etched black against a flamboyant west. Evening came in with flying golden clouds, damp and autumnal, with a smell of earth and leaves as we clustered astern to get the screw 'dug well in' for the last lap.

Wast Hill Tunnel was quite dark with no sign of either end for most of the passage. We were a long time underground as our engine cooling water intake became clogged with leaves causing the engine to over-heat. After some precarious prodding overside in the confined darkness we cleared the intake and came out into a star-canopied night with mist swirling wraith-like from the canal. King's Norton bells were pealing for evensong as I had a last cup of tea with Bob Flint and thanked him for his cooking.

"I'll let you into a secret," he said. "Last night I had no flour, so that parsley sauce was made with custard powder."

Several more trips on NORMAN CHAMBERLAIN sustained my canal interest throughout the winter, but it was the spring of 1952 before I discovered that there is as great a fascination in the canals of a built-up industrial area as in those which meander mid scenes of rural tranquillity. One April morning I was in the Birmingham Science Museum, Newhall Street, when, glancing through a window, I saw a stretch of canal beneath, and before my surprised gaze a boat appeared from below the building and two girls who comprised the crew began working it up a lock. This was my introduction to the Birmingham Canal Navigations, and I lost no time in making contact with the firm of Thomas Clayton (Oldbury) Ltd. whose narrow boats travel the 9½ miles from Junction Wharf, Oldbury, to Nechells Gasworks, to return with crude tar for the Midland Tar Distillers Ltd. Due to a bonus mileage decreeed by ancient canal Acts, tolls for 17 miles are paid over the 9½ miles between the two points. This seeming anomaly arises from the extra work and expense of constructing a mile of canal with locks as against a mile without, and as there is a fall from 470 feet at Oldbury to 300 at Nechells, no fewer than 27 locks are necessary to lower or raise a boat 170 feet. Thus the journey is arduous.

The Birmingham canal system came into being at the end of the eighteenth century. In 1842 a canal carrying business was started by William Clayton, great grandfather of Mr A. H. Clayton, the present manager and director. William died in 1882, one of his sons, Thomas, continuing the business which became a company in 1904. Later, the general goods carrying was merged in Fellows, Morton and Clayton Ltd., but Thomas Clayton (Oldbury) Ltd. retained the carriage of liquids in bulk, with headquarters at Junction Wharf because of its proximity to the tar distillery.

Forrester Clayton, nephew of Thomas, expanded the business and began what is still an important part of the firm's trade, the carrying of fuel and diesel oils from the Manchester Ship Canal to Oldbury. He also set up a depot at Brentford which does canal and estuarial carrying around London. Canal carriage is more economical on the short haul — the additional time being detrimental on longer journeys. Thus hauls between local gasworks and Oldbury form the bulk of the work of Clayton's 90 boats, and last year 150,000 tons of tar products had been carried by them.

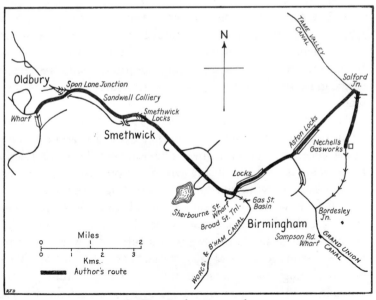

3: Birmingham's canals

A candle-illumined cabin was the only light in the darkness below the bridge at Oldbury as I stumbled down the slope to the towpath just before 4 a.m. and bawled "TOWY ahoy". A dog barked, and a voice answered from an unexpected direction. Clouds of vapour and gleaming lights high on the tar distillery only deepened the gloom at my feet, but with vague watery noises a dark shape materialised as TOWY slid her stern across the canal to offer a bridge, and I went aboard to meet skipper Leslie Berridge. A taciturn man of 35, he had some schooling, went on the canal at 14, and married a boat girl. He thumped the cabin wall.

"Get up you two," he shouted to his daughters, Annie, 13, and Gertie, 12, and we edged along the gunwale to the engine room for'ard of the cabin. There, after a magnificent pyrotechnic display, the 15 h.p. diesel engine sputtered into life and fumes belched from the exhaust which rises above the engine room and adds its discomfort to the smuts which assault the helmsman's eyes from the cabin chimney. TOWY was lying alongside its butty KUBINA, the two narrow boats housing the Berridge family. Mrs Berridge was confined with her new sixth-born, and Johnnie, 5, with Tommy, 3, were also sleeping with her in KUBINA. Annie joined them, leaving Gertie as crew aboard TOWY. Eight-year-old Leslie, having already fallen in the canal 15 times, was now safe at Wood End Hall, the Birmingham Education Committee hostel which gratuitously boards up to 29 canal children during term and sends them to school.

At 4 a.m. we set out, empty, for Nechells Gasworks. A mixed odour of oil, tar, and canal enshrouded us — and a darkness which Leslie's eyes could penetrate but mine could not. Even when light from factories made confusion worse confounded he sorted out water from land with consummate ease. Angles of buildings reflected faithfully in light patches ahead broke into grotesque dances in the disturbed water astern. Past Accles & Pollocks, Simplex, and Chance's Glassworks we puttered. Overhead cranes were lit by furnace beams. Factory canal basins loomed like black caverns, though one momentarily revealed a colourful industrial diorama of red flame and blue radiance, and a glass-sided workshop floated past like a green aquarium. Then the pollarded willows

above a cutting showed as a tracery against a sky already hinting
of dawn, and Gertie made an appearance as we went down the
three Smethwick locks, drinking a cup of tea and nonchalantly
steering the while.

"Watch her put it straight into the lock," said Leslie as TOWY
crossed a short pound, and surely it entered the lock impeccably.
Tangye's, Avery's – Midland industry passed in review. On the
long straight pound through Winson Green I could see well
enough to take the tiller. A bombed mill, once busy with flour
boats, went by on our left, and we came up to our first view of the
city centre, a back view of Wales Cots in Oozells Street, and the
television contraption on top of Telephone House.

Gertie ran ahead at Tindal Bridge with a kettle for water from
a towpath tap. The Worcester Canal went off to our right,
passing beneath the Church of the Messiah, Broad Street, and at
the Crescent Arm we began to descend the 13 Farmer's Bridge
Locks. A windlass in her belt, Gertie took me to the first lock. It
was empty. Raising the nearside paddle adeptly with her windlass,
she rushed to close the bottom gate. Dashing back to the top gate
she raised the centre paddle and crossed the gate to raise the far
one. In a minute the lock was full. Then, leaning our combined
weight on the arm, we ponderously opened the top gate, a job
Gertie normally does alone.

Behind us Leslie brought TOWY into the lock, closed the top
gate and paddles, released the water through the paddles of the
bottom gate, and, when TOWY had dropped to the level of the next
pound, opened it and chugged out. Methodically Gertie and I
pushed and turned our way downhill, under Summer Row at
Saturday Bridge; beneath the Science Museum at Newhall Street;
through the huge railway arch at Snow Hill, and so to the foot of
the locks and an unusual view of St. Chad's Roman Catholic
Cathedral.

"Them locks is Brummagem," Gertie remarked, and, pointing
to the Dental Hospital, "Mum had her teeth out there". This
bright-eyed little girl had had no schooling and could not read or
write. She had never slept in a house or seen the sea though she
regularly did the round trip with TOWY and KUBINA to Ellesmere

Port whence the Berridges return with 44 tons of fuel oil, earning £11 per trip.

Birmingham was waking. Peering through warehouse windows I saw men packing crates; lathes were whirring; fans ejected hot air, dust, and industrial odours on to the canal. Here was a strange beauty, more angular, less colourful than countryside beauty but equally fascinating. Shafts of sunlight striking through arches, the changing shapes of smoke wreaths; sufficient to distract a writer's attention from low bridges which threatened to decapitate him, bridges where the lower brickwork is deeply incised by two centuries of friction from tow ropes. To the boatman there are no bridges, only 'bridge 'oles'.

The Aston Eleven or the Lousy Eleven might equally refer to Aston Villa Football Club according to their current form. To the canal boatman they refer to eleven back-breaking locks. Lock-keeper Parker, who ticks off passing boats on a slate, showed me that a dozen or so boats descend or climb the stair daily, but as many as 77 each way were recorded on February 4th, 1928. Windsor Street Gasworks receded astern. Thimble Mill Lane Bridge, Cuckoo Bridge, and Salford Bridge came and went. From the last of these the canal came to life. Off a boat-building yard we met a Clayton 'black boat' laden with creosote for the General Electric Company. From a hatch on the houseboat CORN IN EGYPT a head enquired of Leslie as to the health of Bill, who was, apparently, still 'on the box'. Then her father called to Gertie below "Here's your Aunty Ivy", and as our boats passed he told his relatives, who ply from Camp Hill Wharf, "We've got a babby now." Following Aunty Ivy was narrow boat GIPPING, a dog in a kennel amidships and Mrs Jinks shaking a mat overside.

So to the gasworks. Our hatches were opened, and within 15 minutes 22 tons of crude tar at 90 degrees Fahrenheit poured from the feeder into our holds.

A mallard drake was swimming around at Nechells as we began our return journey, as gay and exotic as unexpected among rail sidings and power stations. Speed was reduced alongside the wharf as we trawled for coal from the canal bottom, the most profitable five minutes fishing I have ever seen. The outward journey had

taken 4½ hours, reaching a maximum speed of 5 m.p.h. Our
return, working the 27 locks in reverse direction, was to take an
hour longer. Fleeting glimpses from bus tops are the sum of the
townsman's familiarity with Birmingham canals. The canalside
view of a bus is of a momentary view of a red or yellow switch-
back across hump-backed bridges, up, down, and gone. Otherwise this trench through the city is a world apart.

One boat only passed us on our homeward way, an open-boat
with wire coils horse-drawn from Hockley to Powers of Saltley.
But continually we passed through a graveyard of boats: waterlogged, their timbers decayed, their skeletons rusting, dross to the
canal carrier, gold to the scrap merchant. Back at Junction Wharf,
Oldbury, while TOWY disgorged her tar, I warmed my cold body
at a Viking funeral, a roaring fire of narrow boat timbers and the
mast of a butty. But around me, in and on a dozen boats, was
prolific life similar to that of a fair-ground. Laundry billowed
merrily. toddlers frightened my parental heart with their waterside capers, heirs to a separate race which has intermarried and
gone its way for 200 years unchanged. Before you apply ordinary
standards to its upbringing and conditions remember Leslie
Berridge's father-in-law. He wants to return to the boats from his
new house because it is too draughty.

CHAPTER TWO

During an interlude with the B.B.C. aboard
NORMAN CHAMBERLAIN *I collect three more*
canal tunnels, and learn much more about Black
Country canals and boatmen.

When I heard that the B.B.C. was contemplating a cruise of
Midland canals aboard NORMAN CHAMBERLAIN in July 1952, I did
some quick lobbying of the bodies concerned — the Docks &
Inland Waterways Executive, the Birmingham Federation of
Boys' Clubs, and the B.B.C. My relations with all three being
excellent, a request to join in the journey was granted, and I was
left with an embarrassing choice of two whole days out of six, that
being the maximum justifiable to produce the 1,600-word
illustrated article which was my immediate purpose.

Crew and B.B.C. commentators were to gather aboard
NORMAN CHAMBERLAIN at Tardebigge Wharf on Sunday, July
13th, 1952. Monday's journey would bring them up the
Worcester & Birmingham Canal through Tardebigge,
Shortwood, and Wast Hill tunnels, the 'home stretch' familiar to
me from several week-end cruises and familiar to my readers from
my articles. This ruled out the first day. Ultimately I decided on
the second and third days, these taking the cruise from
Birmingham to Coombs Wood, Tipton, Wolverhampton and
Walsall, and including three tunnels as yet unknown to me —
Netherton, Gosty Hill, and Dudley. Thereafter the cruise was
continuing northward towards Cannock and veering westward to
finish at Kinver and Stewpony.

So, on the afternoon of Saturday, July 12th, I helped Paul
Winterforde-Young and John Austin take NORMAN CHAMBERLAIN
from her basin at King's Norton to Tardebigge 10 miles distant,
a journey as beautiful as ever, but noteworthy only for the kingfisher we saw on the Birmingham side of Wast Hill Tunnel.

Godfrey Baseley — founder of 'The Archers' — who was to produce the canal programme, was a passenger.

The B.B.C. was sending its ace commentators, and the next morning, a blustery day, I met Audrey Russell and Wynford Vaughan Thomas as they stepped aboard. Over lunch we warned them of the manifold dangers of canal travel — asphyxiation by carbon monoxide gas in tunnels, decapitation at bridges, and sudden death by drowning. Undeterred, they ate heartily, delighted and relieved to find NORMAN CHAMBERLAIN so habitable, and Tardebigge Wharf so rural. Apart from a new coat of paint the boat was her usual self, with the exception that a door had been fixed to the fore-cabin, normally the quarters of Paul and his second-in-command on boys' cruises. Miss Russell's privacy was to be shared by Win Matthewman, Mr Baseley's secretary, until recently with Wilfred Pickles' 'Have A Go' team.

Paul and John, devoting a week of their holidays to the purpose, were living aboard as crew. Godfrey, who told us that the idea for the broadcasts came several years before when he did a trip on the Shropshire Union Canal, would spend much time aboard, sleeping several nights. As the programmes were to occupy 15 minutes from 6.45 to 7 p.m., Godfrey would have the mortification that listeners to the canal broadcasts would miss 'The Archers', with the times clashing on the Light Programme.

So I left them with Godfrey measuring if it was possible to get a length of cable from the recording car as far as the top lock to reproduce the sound of rushing water, and Wynford and Audrey making their first investigation — in the canal workshops beside the Tardebigge mooring where every possible requirement for the full life afloat is available, even to wallpaper for a homely effect in the cabins.

Although I was not expected aboard on Monday, I had never travelled the Worcester & Birmingham Canal from Selly Oak to the centre of Birmingham, and my curiosity was increased by the tribute in Anne Treneer's *A Stranger in the Midlands* — 'I think the best walk in Birmingham is from Selly Oak to New Street by the bank of the canal. I often walked that way in later years when coltsfoot was golden. I passed the University and distant Queen

Elizabeth Hospital to where fields were green and trees were shapely. By the houses and gardens of once rich city merchants I passed under arches which spanned black water, and which would have been admired if they were in a Belgian city. As houses and factories closed in, I reached a strange place, Dickensian in its picturesque squalor, a medley of heights and shapes. Dickensian indeed it was, for I was near the house of the wharfinger in *Pickwick Papers.*'

So, judging by the itinerary that I would cut off the boat at Lifford Lane at 1 p.m., I waited, and soon it appeared round the bend by King's Norton Factory Centre, passing its own basin, and bearing down on me in the splendour of new paint, red, green, white, and black. I went aboard just as Lifford Salvage Works, nodding across at the canal sidings and railway, were convincing the two commentators that industry had at last taken command of the sylvan waterway of the morning. They were now in canal

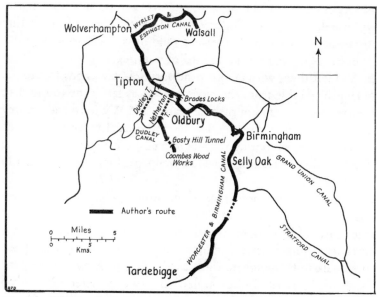

4: The Birmingham Canal Navigations and Shropshire Union Canal

garb, Audrey wearing navy slacks and beret and Wynford in golf
jacket, drill slacks, and plimsolls; and they had experienced their
baptism of fire, or rather water, in Wast Hill Tunnel.

Soon we had Cadbury's Bournville Works on our left with
their loading wharfs on our right. The late George Cadbury was
a keen advocate of inland waterways traffic, and the name is often
on the lips of boatmen who have carried goods from Cadbury's
factories at Frampton on the Gloucester & Berkeley Canal, and at
Knighton on the 'Shroppy'.

"I feel like a Bisto kid," said Audrey, inhaling the chocolate
smell. So spontaneously did she mix her culinary metaphor that I
was left wondering how B.B.C. people avoid lapses into ad-
vertising.

At Elliott's Metal Company, Selly Oak, the travellers made
their first acquaintance with the openings into factory basins.
Today Elliott's openings are blocked, but I remember in 1926
when I worked there awhile on my first job from school, that at
least two canal boats daily drew into covered arms in the factory
to take sheet metal to various railway stations. We were to be
joined at Selly Oak bridge by two important visitors, James
Oxley, Divisional Traffic Officer of the South-Western Division
of the D.I.W.E., and Harvey J.Dunkerley, Controller of the
Midland Region, B.B.C. They were waiting just beyond the
junction with the Dudley Canal at Birmingham Battery Company
— two respectable gentlemen in lounge suits and trilbies, Mr
Oxley even wearing a yellow carnation. The Dudley Canal is now
disused from the Lappal Tunnel having caved in.

We pursued our placid way past the red brick pile of the
University and the darker bulk of the Queen Elizabeth Hospital.
On the railway beside us the 'Pines Express' and 'The Devonian'
rushed past. As we approached Edgbaston and chugged beneath its
short tunnel, industry was again left behind and a canopy of trees
waved from one bank, while on the other we had open views of
spacious residences and school playing fields. I found myself in
agreement with Anne Treneer. This was pleasant countryside to
within three minutes of Birmingham centre, for we had scarcely
come up against the towering walls of the Accident Hospital and

its neighbouring brewery when we arrived at Worcester Bar in Gas Street Basin.

Here broadcasting history was made. We were immediately below Broadcasting House, Broad Street — indeed Pearce and Cutler's arm lapped its very walls. For the first time B.B.C. commentators had arrived at the studio by water. The occasion merited a press photograph which I arranged, and Mr Oxley made a recording for that night's programme. Then on, under Broad Street Tunnel, where Birmingham's waterway to the south-west joins its artery to the north-west. A group of small girls begged to be taken aboard, and our refusal led them to express the uncharitable hope that we might 'bash our blinkin' 'eads in' on the tunnel roof. But by now we were all adept at avoiding just that fate.

As NORMAN CHAMBERLAIN nosed into Sherbourne Street Wharf we were the object of considerable ill-informed comment from workers through factory windows and from other vantage points.

'How much a week, mate?' 'Blimey, wot a soft job!' 'Want a secretary?' The pleasant job isn't necessarily the lazy one. We had enjoyed our trip, but I, for one, had not been idle, and I had to go home to several hours typing. I am a veritable Atlas of a scribbler, and as I was to see during the two following days, Audrey and Wynford were doing a 16-hours' day, pleasant enough perhaps, but wearing nerve, sinew, and imagination, and in conditions which did not allow the best of sleep o' nights.

So I left NORMAN CHAMBERLAIN tied up among the blue and yellow boats of British Waterways, some disgorging spelter ingots which had come to Birmingham from the Pacific coast of Canada, all the way by water. And Mr Oxley was pointing up the canal, sparkling in afternoon sunshine, and saying to Wynford, "That's the main line to Liverpool."

Having risen at 5.30 next morning I went aboard NORMAN CHAMBERLAIN to be greeted by Programme Parade after the 7 o'clock News: 'Paul Winterforde-Young and John Austin will need all their skill today to navigate NORMAN CHAMBERLAIN to Halesowen and Tipton.' They seemed in no way daunted by the responsibility, but any private doubts they may have harboured

were soon dispelled by the arrival of Fred Moore with his boss
Ernie Thomas, owner of 300 boats plying from Birchills Old
Wharf near Walsall.

Fred was to join the crew for the rest of the week as navigator.
Burly, baldish, and born on the canal at Wolverhampton 43 years
ago, he knew the Midlands waterways like the back of his hand,
and was bringing up his sons in the same tradition. His 15-year-old
was taking charge of the tug DOT in Fred's absence, cruising up to
Cannock Chase collieries from Old Birchills to bring back a train
of three or four butties each carrying 25 to 30 tons of coal for
Walsall Power Station. The return journey takes seven hours, and
DOT tows some 600 tons of coal each week. Fred had married off
the canal ('one of the townsolk', he described his wife) and had
gone to live on the wharf at Birchills in order to send his boys to
school.

"I never went to school," he told me, "but I'm happy with my
life. My boys have schooling. It's very nice, but I don't miss it."

Some writers would succumb to the temptation to put tongue
in cheek and philosophize on peace of mind, inward content, and
the true values. I happen to think that academic education is of
value in itself, but Fred turned out to be a grand bloke, and I'll
leave the last word with Wynford: 'I've met more happy people
on canals than anywhere.' Audrey had spent the night ashore and
would meet us around mid-day, but our numbers were increased
by photographer John Turnbull and B.B.C. engineer Desmond
O'Leary, an old friend, who shipped as cook but commenced
operations by asking me if one fries eggs or bacon first if both
cannot be done together.

In the morning sunshine we headed out to the long straight
reach through Winson Green alongside the railway as local trains
carried office workers to their desks, and doubtless they, too,
dismissed us as 'good time Charlies'. One horse-drawn narrow
boat passed us, and another, heading for Birmingham, both of the
firm of Thomas Clayton (Oldbury) Ltd.

"Marnin' Fred," said a wizened old crone at the tiller of the
second, and Fred gave us a running commentary on the helmsmen
as boats became more frequent.

"That's old George, seventy he be, worked on the cut all his life."

"Ben there's never slept in anything but a canal boat and him nigh on seventy". Seventy seems an average age for canal boatmen. We took the right-hand turn where Sandwell Gospel Hall, high on the bank, flaunts its fearsome texts well known to all rail travellers between Birmingham and Wolverhampton. Boatmen who are illiterate miss nothing but a laugh in their inability to read of such hellfire and damnation.

"That's a better canalside sign," said John Turnbull as we passed 'The Boatman Inn — Mitchells & Butlers'.

"Yo're a-gooin' up a dead end," bawled some facetious kids ashore. Cruising under two fine bridges, one dated 1790, we slowed down to pass Sandwell Colliery, where a dozen boats were tied up to receive coal from the chute. "How's your mother?" asked one of the boatmen of Fred. These people of the canals are a race apart, much inter-bred, and knowing one another from Ellesmere Port on the Shropshire Union to Brentford on the Grand Union.

As we approached Oldbury our view, which had been restricted by the walls of factories rising from the canal, opened out and Wynford saw his first panorama of the Black Country, dominated by Dudley Castle above its tree-clad slopes. With canals having played so prominent a part in the development of Black Country industry it was only right that the canal should become populous at this juncture. On Spon Lane Aqueduct, where we crossed over the Birmingham Level and a railway passed over us, we nosed carefully past an old man, with a cloth cap and corduroys strapped below the knees, who was 'shafting' two boats full of steel rails — moving them himself from the towing path with a long pole. He would take them thus a mile or more to the District Iron & Steel Works.

Wynford had gone below to change from canal garb to gent's natty suiting, ready to be received at Accles & Pollocks. Passing Clayton's yard in the shadow of Midland Tar Distillers Ltd., Fred encountered a storm of backchat from the assembly of boats always found there. Bridges now had names — Seven Stars might well have lived up to its own had I not ducked quickly, and at High Bridge, a shocking misnomer, my heart missed a beat as I pressed down hard against the saloon roof and even so shaved my most prominent protuberance — the seat of my trousers. Near here Paul pointed out Element's boatyard where he had found NORMAN CHAMBERLAIN, a derelict hulk like several still lying there. Around us were other boats, belonging to J. & S. Tonks, with an unusual design, not unlike a bird's-eye view of a turtle in red spreading over the closed double doors and outer wall of the cabin. It occurred again on one or two boats belonging to William Cresswell, whom I met alongside Accles & Pollocks Wharf. We had tied up outside his PEARL, named after a three-year-old grand-daughter, to let Wynford go ashore, and while a constant stream of workers came to look at NORMAN CHAMBERLAIN I chatted with William in that friendly canal fashion engendered when one's floating home lies adjacent to another for a while.

Mr Cresswell's first impulse was to vacate his berth so that we might pull up against the wharf, thus saving the Accles & Pollocks moguls the hazards of a Blondin act over his crossbars when they returned with Wynford to inspect our boat. I managed to dissuade him. What had been good enough for an ace B.B.C. commentator to go ashore was good enough for industrialists to come aboard. Mr Cresswell is only a small boat-owner, with two motor-boats, four open boats, and a dredger, and business is bad. Fifteen years ago he brought 15 boats weekly to Accles & Pollocks; now he brings four or five. His cargo is coal and washed slack from Conduit Collieries, Norton Canes, and he has spent his last 34 years on this run. Prior to that he regularly 'legged' through Dudley Tunnel. Like so many boatmen he was born on the canal — at Lee Brook, Wednesbury, on a George Griffiths boat which carried cargoes to London.

As we chatted, we were liberally bespattered with a coating of black smuts from Accles chimneys and dust from the washed slack unloading from other boats, brought direct from the collieries. Coal has always been among the most important cargoes carried by canal, and indeed, when domestic coal first came into Birmingham by water its price fell from 13 shillings a ton to 8s.4d. It is

recorded: 'On the 6th of November 1769, the first boat-load of
coals ever brought into Birmingham by canal was conveyed into
the town. Crowds of people went to see it. There was a sort of
holiday kept on the occasion. Bonfires blazed on the wharfs, bands
of music played, and there was something like general rejoicing.'

Other times, other cargoes. Coal still plies by canal, particularly
to the new electricity power stations, but oil and petroleum fill
many bottoms today. Two of Clayton's horse-drawn boats passed
by on the last lap of a three or four day journey from Ellesmere
Port. Each carried 25 tons of oil, and the same horses would have
pulled all the way. In each case a little girl, aged perhaps 13 and
small as these canal children seem to be, led the horse which was
gay with coloured spoles on his harness to prevent cutting. Bound
northward Clayton's TAY with its butty PEEL set us rocking in its
wash as it set out for Ellesmere Port and Manchester Ship Canal.

Wynford had changed back into his canal gear as we locked
down Brades Hall Locks — three of them, to bring us to the
Birmingham Level. Here we had the first of many gifts, Mrs King
who lived in the lock house presenting us with a huge lettuce from
her garden. An unseen cow was lowing from a shed behind her
home, and before us stretched our first close-up glimpse of the
tortured sterile face of the Black Country, uninhabited and
uninhabitable, with tiny hillocks, which owed more to man than
nature, rising from an unstable base.

We soon saw man changing the face of the land, a party of canal
workers on a dredger transferring shining black mud from the
canal bottom to the canal side, where time would soon clothe it
with mugwort, hairy willow-herb and coltsfoot. It was while we
were discussing canalside flora that we were introduced to
Wynford's bedside book for the cruise, *Fleas, Flukes, and Cuckoos*
in the New Naturalist series, a volume on parasites and apparently
a monument of out-of-the-way research and a mine of unsuspected
information.

We turned left into the Birmingham Level, and while chugging
parallel with the main Birmingham – Wolverhampton railway
we had a few horrible moments when we disturbed a wild duck
and her brood. At first they swam off in orderly line astern before

us, six waddling ducklings behind their mother. But it became obvious that we were overtaking them and panic set in. First one, then another of the babies submerged, until only mother was left flapping awkwardly ahead. We shouted to John Austin to cut the engine, but it was a while before he heard, and we watched anxiously in our wake, fearing to see some mangled little bodies churned up by the screw. As our speed slackened, Mrs Duck regained confidence and took wing, flying in a wide half circle whence she had come. Soon she could be seen fussing round the ducklings who seemed unharmed.

When man rends the ground as he has done in the Black Country, it sometimes hits back to confound him. On our left hereabouts was a deep pit of considerable extent, into which the slopes, covered with bleached grass, disappeared beneath our range of vision. A narrow brick culvert slanted steeply down with them from the canal bank. This was the scene on 'the ninth of the ninth, ninety nine', as canal men put it, just as we used to talk of the 'eleventh hour of the eleventh day of the eleventh month'.

Here Barnett's Breach took place between three and four of a Saturday morning on September 9th, 1899. Only the narrow towpath separated the canal from a marl-hole which fell away beside it to a depth of 300 feet. Suddenly 100 yards of the towpath caved in, and the canal began emptying itself through the chasm into the pit. Two iron boats full of ashes were swept through the gap and hurtled down with the torrent — they belonged to Samuel Barnett, whose Rattle Chain & Stour Valley Brick Works obtained their clay from the marl pit, in which the water was now rapidly rising as it fell away up the reach of canal towards Dudley Port northwards and Albion to the south.

One boat plying nearby began to race for the breach, and only by jumping out and cutting the tow-rope was the boatman able to save himself and his horse. Another; near Dudley Port Station, accelerated its pace to overtake the horse, who followed at an increasing canter. Again the boatman scrambled ashore and managed to get a rope secure round a telegraph pole, thus arresting his boat's headlong career.

The *Birmingham Post* of Monday, September 11th, 1899, in the course of a graphic report said 'Some idea may be gained of the terrible rush of water by the fact that the marl-hole, although 100 yards deep and having a surface boundary of three acres, was quickly filled to the brim, whilst nearly two acres of surrounding meadows were submerged.' Soon two miles of canal were completely drained, and six miles, including arms, lay muddy and lowered in depth. An inspector and his gang arrived and the lock gates were closed at Ryder's Green, a mile towards Birmingham, and also above the breach at Factory Locks, Tipton. Wooden planks were fixed across the canal to impound what water was left in them. In Netherton Tunnel the level was lowered considerably. Ultimately, traffic on 30 or 40 miles of canal had to be diverted, the Dudley Tunnel being pressed into service.

Telegraphic communication between Dudley and Birmingham was impeded through poles being swept away. Damage to canal property was estimated at between £40,000 and £50,000, while Mr Barnett claimed that it would cost him between £3,000 and £4,000. To pump water out of the pit alone cost £500. At Rattle Chain Works and at Stour Valley Works 150 and 100 workers were temporarily unemployed. A hundred thousand sightseers visited the scene of chaos on the Sunday, and local youths were soon busy scouring the canal bottom for coal which had fallen from boats over a long period.

Naturally each side disclaimed responsibility for the calamity. Mr Barnett asserted that his men had been aware of a leak from the canal into the marl-hole for some time. The Birmingham Canal Company claimed that not only was the embankment weakened by blasting in the marl-hole, but that smouldering ashes dumped by the brickworks helped loosen the tenacity of the puddle dam of clay which extended three feet thick along the complete length of the level. Barnett's Breach was the most serious ever experienced in the Black Country though there had been one some years before at Deepfields, again into a marl-hole which belonged to Sir Alfred Hickman.

Another left turn at Netherton Tunnel Junction, and NORMAN CHAMBERLAIN was heading for the Rowley Hills across a landscape of derelict mine workings and brick works. Soon the tunnel appeared ahead, the canal continuing its undeviating course into the hillside. We passed beneath an aqueduct carrying the Wolverhampton Level, and through Netherton Gauging Station, where a bunch of young onions sent overland by Mrs King to supplement her lettuce was handed to us. A tug was emerging from the tunnel as we entered, towing a string of Stewart & Lloyd's boats, and its smoke provided us with a most remarkable tunnel effect. It blotted out the preternaturally clear view along the canal which one usually gets from a tunnel as though looking through a telescope, and dimmed the daylight to a ruddy orange glow with just the gauging station, in the middle of the canal with a channel on either side, framed in the opening like the backcloth to a sinister stage set.

As the smoke cleared, the clarity returned, but we were too far into the tunnel to see much and were more interested in the exit which was looming larger in front, looking first like the semi-circle of white lights one often sees above the entrance to a fairground, but changing to a wheatsheaf shape as we approached near enough to see the reflection of the opening. Netherton Tunnel, 3027 yards long, was the last of our English canal tunnels to be built, being started in December 1855 and completed within three years. There are towpaths with handrails on either side, and the tunnel is unique in its electric light, though this is far from brilliant. The headroom is 15 ft 9 ins, and the width, including towpaths, 27 ft. There are eight concentric rings of brickwork lining the tunnel before the rough rock and clay is reached. As the bricks are 4½ inches in depth this gives 36 inches thickness of brickwork, with two more inches of mortar. It is a fairly dry tunnel, but the reflection of the damp brick arch in the still waters near the end gives a perfect impression of the round barrel of brick through which the canal flows.

The greatest depth below the land surface is about 250 feet, and there are five open ventilation shafts — the fourth from Halesowen end coming up in the middle of a roundabout in Sycamore Road, Tividale — and seven temporarily sealed, which could be opened up to remove debris in the event of a fall. In 1907 a 'bump' occurred in mid-tunnel, the ground rising three feet and

leaving only 2 ft 6 inches of water. Again this maltreated soil of the
Black Country was hitting back. Miners used to work to within
100 yards of the tunnel.

Our passage took nearly 40 minutes and we emerged into a
landscape of the tortured earth which, now mercifully overgrown, is not unpleasant. The hillside above the tunnel was a
gentle slope of unenclosed pasture studded with hawthorn bushes.
Below ground were the disused workings of Warren Hall and
Windmill End No. 3 pits. At Windmill End Junction the bricked
canal banks have continually to be lifted because of the unstable
nature of the subsoil. A short distance down the Netherton Lodge
Farm canal a pub, 'The Wheatsheaf' stood, gradually
disintegrating until about 1925 came the final cataclysm, and the
site is now uneven and empty. An arm stretched, reed-fringed,
into a wilderness of willow-herb towards where Windmill End
No. 3 pit once disgorged its coat. Now, to my surprise, a solitary
fisherman disturbed it. Apparently he could expect quite good
sport.

We took the canal to the left, leading to Gosty Hill Tunnel and
the Coombs Wood Works of Stewart & Lloyds. Beside the junction a symmetrical spoil heap rose near a derelict pump-house
which once pumped water from the mine. Pink blossoms of
willow-herb clustered deep where once was a scene of industry.
Among the reeds in a dead-end canal, once Warren Hall basin, lay
the black bones of a narrow boat.

Wynford was astounded by the wide panorama of Black
Country before him. 'Fantastic,' he said more than once. From
the jagged teeth of Rowley quarries which appeared to be closing
on houses on the skyline, the haphazard man-made landscape
stretched below and around us, rows of houses, factories,
railways, pylons, smoke, gasworks, canal, barren ground,
brickworks, and a church on a hilltop. But behind it all were the
gracious hill silhouettes of Clent and Walton, as yet immune from
the assault of industry.

Our presence was becoming known. From every bridge groups
waved at us or they accompanied us along the towpath. At each
bridge we delayed our scuttle for the fore-hatch just long enough

to wave back and exchange some of the banter. And dangerous the bridges were — Alkali Bridge, Dog Lane Bridge, and many others with little headroom. Indeed, an old man toddled alongside and, in no way reassured by our safe, if tight, passage beneath each succeeding bridge, predicted certain calamity at the next. Paul came nearest to trouble when, losing his nerve at the prospect of a very tight squeeze, he jumped to his feet at the very last minute and raced the bridge along the length of the boat, going desperately to earth in the engine room just in time.

As we glided through the Gawn housing estate it was obvious we were expected. We saw word of our coming precede us down the line of back doors. Women left their housework and children their play to gaze, one woman even to wave a Union Jack which got her a mention in that night's broadcast. If the towpath and bridges were populous the canal was not.

"Twenty-five years ago you had to be a boatman on this stretch," said Mr G. W. King, general canal foreman, who was travelling with us. "It was crowded with boats."

Mr King started work on the canal as a bricklayer's labourer aged 14 in 1921, when he had to cycle from Walsall to Halesowen daily to work. He came of a canal family — father and grandfather had served before him. We were joined by another canal character to take us through Gorsty Hill Tunnel, Jack Brownhill, who has worked a tug through the tunnel for 26 years and claims to have pulled such trains that he has been half-a-mile away when the last boat cleared the tunnel. His cargoes included steel tubes, coal, chemicals, oils, and spelter. Twenty-five years ago a boatman would take a load of 25 tons of Rowley road stone from Rowley quarries to Birmingham collecting depots and return as one day's job.

At sight of the portal of the tunnel I realised the reason for ballasting NORMAN CHAMBERLAIN well down. Would she possibly clear that small hole? I'd been in bigger sewers. We were all rather apprehensive, Paul most of all, an apprehension which became a lively fear for the boat as she forced her nose into the darkness. I crouched on the forepeak with several others, our hair and ears almost scraping the slimy bricks. We fended her bows off as best

we could — no easy task as there was no room to spare. At reduced
speed we crept along the 557 yards length, for all the world like
cruising along a sewer, even to the rather close atmosphere from
the warm water which runs in at Stewart & Lloyds. In his
broadcast at night Wynford described the journey as feeling "like
being squeezed through a tube of toothpaste", than which further
comment is superfluous.

Proserpine, when she returned from the underworld, had no
reception to compare with ours at Stewart & Lloyds as NORMAN
CHAMBERLAIN materialized from the darkness into their Coombs
Wood Works. Our coming coincided with dinner time and a
thousand or so of the workers were on the canal side, on roofs, at
windows, occupying any vantage point. As we tied up one boiler-
suited figure nudged me and jerked his thumb upwards and across
the canal.

"'E's bin tryin' to get out for foar years," he said. I looked up
at a tiny window with bars, where the antics of a fat man as he
tried to wave might have been desperate attempts to escape from
prison. Around us were boats with steel tubes for Rhodesia,
Transvaal, and Iran. The pipelines of Iraq begin their journey to
the desert on the canal at Coombs Wood.

Wynford, changed for a second time into his 'natty suiting',
went to look round the factory and later to visit Doulton's glazed
pottery works. Audrey came aboard, and as she had lunch autograph books were thrust through the windows for her signature.
While she dictated script to Win during the afternoon we cruised
back through Gosty Hill and Netherton tunnels to the
Birmingham Level, where we turned left on our final lap beside
the railway with Mond's Gas Works towering above us. So up
through the three Factory Locks at Tipton Gauging Station, and
into the basin where we tied up around teatime for the evening
broadcast and to stay the night.

There was no doubt NORMAN CHAMBERLAIN was now one of the
sights of the Black Country. Crowds gathered while we had tea,
and a B.B.C. recording car added to the excitement. The good
people of Tipton turned up in their hundreds with autograph
books. John Austin thoughtfully carried the boat's radio to a wall

alongside the basin, and while the actual broadcast was done in the office of the gauging station the crowd stood outside and listened.

The broadcast over, the autograph hunters swooped. While, of course, Wynford and Audrey were the main attraction, Godfrey Baseley as producer of 'The Archers' was rated a good third. But none of us in the boat was spared, and I signed my undistinguished name a hundred times if once. Wynford, escaping at last, grinned at me and said: "Just to think I used to object to 50 lines at school."

When the others had gone to take their ease at an inn Paul and I remained behind on NORMAN CHAMBERLAIN and had a visit from a lively crowd of girls and boys, members of a Tipton youth club.

If there is a more matey place than NORMAN CHAMBERLAIN made snug for the night I don't know it, and this night it excelled. Wynford lying on his mattress, his top half protruding from the blankets inadequately covered by a silk primrose garment with huge red and green fishes, which he excused by saying that it was a present from the US Navy at Honolulu on his epic round the world flight in eight days, read to us extracts on the more intimate life of the flea from *Fleas, Flukes, and Cuckoos*. We roared with laughter, which brought a gentle protest from Audrey's cabin where her literary nightcap was Cecil Woodham Smith's *Florence Nightingale*. Paul, being transported from a canal at Tipton to sterner boatmanship on *The Kon-Tiki Expedition*, was louder in his opposition. But one by one we dropped off to sleep; Wynford's succeeding extracts had a diminishing audience, and finally he too slept, untroubled by the parasites about which he had been reading.

If there is any more realistic imitation of an alarm-clock than a lock paddle rattling down, I've never heard it. A succession of such noises suggested considerable traffic on the canal early next morning, and though my natural curiosity drew me from my blankets at 5.30, it was to find Godfrey already at large, dressing-gown over his pyjamas, talking to boatmen as they dropped down the locks. This early rising gave me an opportunity to get on with some of the writing which was my purpose on the cruise. This I did sitting in Godfrey's car after making a brew of tea.

The next sign of life was Audrey tripping with soap, towel, and toothbrush into the adjacent cottage of Sam Robinson who, with true Black Country courtesy, had offered to her and Win the hospitality of his ablutions. Audrey returned some time later carrying a bunch of gypsophila, veronica, and red rambling roses most tastefully grouped. Sam had cut them from his own little garden, and they certainly gave Audrey more pleasure than the costliest of hothouse exotics on more formal occasions. Sam was enjoying his pension after 52 years with the canal company, still living in canal property. It was a reflection on the general conception of the 'bargee' as the hardest swearing of mortals, to learn that when Sam entered the company's employ at the age of 13, boiling tea for the bricklayers, a recommendation from the parson was a normal qualification for employment.

After breakfast Wynford and I had a date with the old Dudley Tunnel, though not in NORMAN CHAMBERLAIN which would have fared badly in the encounter. We drove from our mooring in Godfrey's car with the wooded crest of Wren's Nest on our right. Wynford swore he could now smell a canal a mile away and recognise a canal bridge infallibly. There was no doubt about the bridge when we reached it, and as the canal made straight for the hill it suggested the possibility of a tunnel. But of smell it had none.

We clambered down from the main Birmingham – Wolverhampton road to a path worn through the tall dank grasses and hairy willow-herb, and followed it towards a large boat waiting at the mouth of the tunnel which bears an inscription 'Built 1790'. This was limestone water, cold and clear; prolific in plant life as a Wiltshire chalk stream. We looked down on the waving tree-tops of an under-water jungle. Tadpoles and stickle-backs wriggled or darted among the fronds.

It might have been considered a bad omen as we stood at Castle Mill End beside the mouth of the tunnel that a small dog began to take an unfortunate interest in our camera case and had to be firmly discouraged. Was there not something about giving 'a sop to Cerberus' — the canine guardian of the Underworld? But as two Charons waited to conduct us on our Stygian journey in place of the regulation one perhaps we should win through. We were to venture underground in an open boat. In its empty iron shell Joe Chilton, wearing a red beret and khaki pullover, and Ernie Fenton in Black Country uniform of shirt sleeves and waistcoat, busied themselves with buckets and acetylene containers. One was set up on the forepeak, one amidships on a cross bar, and a third astern. A match was applied and our illumination for the journey came to hissing life.

Five of us vaulted aboard, Mr King the canal foreman, Wynford, John Turnbull with his camera, Desmond — his cooking handed over to Win — and me. Behind us a stop-lock was closed to prevent our being sucked willy-nilly out of the tunnel with the opening of sluices on the canal at Tipton. Joe and Ernie took up their staves and we were off, 'legging' into the heart of Castle Hill. Canal 'legging' is an all-embracing term. Actually our 'leggers' pushed with short staves in nicks in the tunnel brickwork, walking the boat forward beneath them until, stopped by the first crossbar they returned to the forepeak, found more nicks, and repeated their walk. As the legs took the strain perhaps 'legging' was a fair description.

Mr King cheered us by explaining that it is unsafe for a motor-boat to attempt Dudley Tunnel for fear the chugging dislodges chunks of limestone. The rock used to be 'pricked' annually and loose pieces removed — a practice discontinued with less traffic passing.

A few hundred yards brought us into Castle Mill Basin, a spectacular crater in the limestone. Before this we had passed under a circular shaft up which could be seen a stout ceiling. That ceiling is the living-room floor of the Guttridge home, once an engine-house for pumping water from the limestone workings, its coal being brought into the tunnel by boat and delivered up the shaft. Mrs Guttridge will raise her carpet to show a ringed stone in the floor which once gave access to the shaft.

In Castle Mill Basin are some disused lie-bys, arms where boats could pull in out of the way. Here also is the blocked arch of Wren's Nest Tunnel which extends over two miles into the hill, a cul-de-sac constructed as the miners hewed their limestone.

This tunnel made a safe ammunition dump in the First World War.

We scrambled out of Castle Mill crater with its tortured tree roots and beetling crags past a sewer and storm pipe which span the rift, and up to the jumble of hollows and hillocks which denote the work of man before nature resumed sway. Here are magnificent straight ash trunks, thrusting from the depressions into the sunlight to compete with their more favoured neighbours on the mounds. Down into Seven Sisters Cave we slithered on twigs and treacherous limestone mud. The mining followed closely that of coal, parallel roads being cut into the lime strata and joined by regular transverse passages, thus leaving supporting pillars. Seven such limestone buttresses constituted the Seven Sisters, but one has collapsed. Big Ben, Little Ben, and the Lion's Den are local boys' names for other caves; the Bottle Cave and Cherry Hole are more authentic.

There are the '144 Steps' down which I have since scrambled, thick among enchanters nightshade. Down them 83-year-old Mrs Ellen Hall of Castle Mill House remembers walking in her wedding year, 1892, to a dance in a ballroom hewn from the limestone — the old gas brackets can still be seen down there. Gondolas plied on the canal in those days. Now the way is fraught with danger, July and August being the most hazardous months in the caves as the big range of temperature causes rock falls. My explorations have embraced both months.

Back in the boat we pushed into the tunnel proper — Long Rock, a water-paved cavern glittering crystal-like in our flares. Next came Short Tunnel with an arm lapping the Seven Sisters, up which a sunken boat is said to lie; then Long Tunnel, a barrel-shaped conduit of brick half filled with six feet of water, the other six feet left to us. Slowly we creaked along to the hiss and whine of the acetylene and the occasional gurgle of a dislodged rock. The greatest risk was to our fingers, for inadvertently to grasp the sides of the boat was to have them crushed between the hull and the tunnel wall. Ahead, in this long unchanging sewer, was a hollow sound of running water. Dudley Tunnel is a fairly dry one, but at one point a steady flow percolated through, being directed down the sides by galvanised sheets, though enough fell on us to douse a flare. There being no room for boats to pass in the width of 8 ft 6 inches, mid-tunnel encounters were avoided by admitting boats only at 10 a.m. at Tipton end and 2 p.m. at Park Head, the far end.

When we had been more than an hour underground and were about half way, we could see a glimmer of light at each end, but we seemed to make no appreciable progress towards our destination. So I challenged Wynford to a 'push-o-war', and dispossessing Joe and Ernie of their staves we set to, shoving not only in nicks but in the 'buoyat holes' left deliberately to fix planks across the tunnel in repair work. For one mad spell all seven of us pushed with staves and hands, and the boat shot along 'towing the darkness behind us' in Wynford's picturesque phrase used during that night's broadcast. But we had still to negotiate 'The Gaol', a section so narrow that a steel-hulled boat distorted by cargoes of hot metal billets sometimes stuck. Scraping, swearing, and cheering we made it, leaving behind the one air shaft which debouches in an allotment behind Wellington Road. Soon we could distinguish figures in the opening.

"I'll bet Godfrey's there with a stop-watch," said Wynford. "Working with him's like being harnessed to a circular saw."

So we glided into the daylight, and there, among a small crowd, was Godfrey Baseley — with stop-watch in hand. Emerging from the tenebrous earth after two hours underground we preened ourselves and felt an affinity with all pioneers. I even quoted Keats on stout Cortes and his men looking around in wild surmise 'Silent as on a peak in Darien.'

"How long since the last boat came through?" we asked Mr King.

"We brought the ice-boat through yesterday to clear any obstructions," he answered. "Before that nothing had passed since the Sunday School party in May."

Sadly deflated we hung our diminished heads and Godfrey jumped aboard brandishing his stop-watch. "You're late," he told us. "Wynford was due at Monmore Green 15 minutes ago." Wynford gave the wry smile of a man who had been proved correct but wished he hadn't. "What did I tell you?" he said.

It was not always Sunday School treats and inquisitive journalists in Dudley Tunnel. Until two years ago the tunnel was the domain of Jack Wheeler, deceased within this twelve months. For 7s.6d full, and 5s. empty he was legging boats though past his seventieth year. The Harts Hill Iron Co. Ltd. sent five boats weekly until, in August 1950, they closed their Top Side Forge. Before their Old Side Forge closed in February 1928, four or five boats daily made the passage from Harts Hill with cinder residue from iron making for the blast furnaces of Alfred Heaton. They returned with fuel — washed nuts from Hamstead Colliery. From Harts Hill Works to the tunnel mouth the boats were steered for many years by three generations of the Mullett family — Enoch, David, and Luther, resounding Black Country names. Luther still lives beside the canal though he now drives an overhead crane at Round Oak Works. At the tunnel Jack Wheeler took over, to surrender the boats to other custodians at Castle Mill end. Within the last two years Harts Hill works have sold their 28 canal boats to Stewart & Lloyds, Halesowen.

Four hundred yards beyond the Park Head portal the reed-fringed canal branches. The leftward arm drops down four locks, thence to Brierley Hill and through more locks to the Stewpony and usefulness. To the right the Pensnett Canal winds a final mile of decay, past Harts Hill Works to a dead end at The Wallows beneath the smoke pall of Round Oak Works.

Mr George Wood, who has directed canal transport from Harts Hill Works for many years, and fervently desires a return to prosperity of the canals, showed me two iron boats loading with 'scale', 60 to 80 per cent iron content, for Bilston. They would travel via Netherton Tunnel, double the distance through the old Dudley Tunnel. Water plantain and arrowhead poked above the canal surface and innumerable jack-bannocks played around. The Round Oak Fishing Club has recently stocked these waters which were once busy with traffic.

Godfrey took us in his car at Park Head End, and we rejoined NORMAN CHAMBERLAIN at Monmore Green Wharf, Wolverhampton, where Wynford was collared by the directors of Jones, Baylis & Jones, before he had time either to wash off his tunnel grime or to discard his canal garb in favour of more appropriate dress. Stories of a triumphal progress during our absence greeted us from those aboard NORMAN CHAMBERLAIN. We were told of cheering crowds on towpaths, of more flowers for Audrey, and of classes of schoolchildren waiting at vantage points along the route. Indeed, there was still a class from Ettingshall Junior School ranged along the towpath on the opposite side of the canal, and when we cast off I would not have been their teacher for untold riches as his charges followed us over part of our route. However, no one fell in, and they waved their good-byes as they marched in orderly pairs up to a bridge.

We were now on the Wolverhampton Level, hemmed in again by high walls and the backs of factories, cruising through what that excellent canal writer L.T.C. Rolt describes as 'malodorous canyons'. A green-painted bridge bore the legend 'E tenebris oritur lux, 1897', and there we turned back over our tracks and made for Walsall along the Wyrley & Essington Canal.

It was on this stretch that I began my great imposture. Audrey was now missing, having stayed ashore and gone by car to await us at our destination — Walsall Power Station. With Wynford making up arrears of sleep below, NORMAN CHAMBERLAIN was like *Hamlet* without the Prince of Denmark or Ophelia. The audience was there however, at every bridge, at every cluster of houses backing on the cut, and at every factory we passed. Sitting on the roof with notebook and pencil I suppose I looked like a B.B.C. commentator recording his impressions. So, bashfully at first, but with increasing confidence, I acknowledged the waving and cheers, hoping that no one would expose me by bawling a direct question as to my identity. I had the grace to blush when one workman observed loudly to his mates, pointing at me, "That bloke flew round the world in eight days."

As we approached one family group at their garden fence which backed on the towpath, an old lady piped up "Where's Miss Russell, please?" I explained as we drew abreast that she was not aboard. The old lady looked disappointed and uncertain what to do with a large orange.

"I hoped Miss Russell would accept this," she said. A gap was

opening between us and she was not a very robust lady. It would
be shocking anti-climax, not only for her to miss Audrey, but for
her orange to fall short and bob behind us in the murky waters.
But I took a chance and asked her to throw it. With a precision
many county cricketers would have envied she tossed the orange
towards NORMAN CHAMBERLAIN. The gap was now considerable,
but it was so good a throw that I did not even have to rise. As I
caught the orange, Wynford's head popped out of a hatchway. I
gave him the orange with instructions to pass it to Audrey. That
night one old lady was doubtless delighted to hear Audrey's
thanks during the broadcast.

At Pinfold Bridge, Wednesfield, where one of the biggest
crowds had collected, including the local day nursery, we jumped
ashore to visit 'The Dog & Partridge', a pub immortalised in Phil
Drabble's *Black Country,* where the landlord stands among his
customers to pull the beer instead of behind a bar. Back aboard we
had one of those wonderful lunches provided by the B.B.C.
catering department. We were travelling along a relatively lonely
stretch of canal, and as I stood in the galley washing-up, a boy
attracted my attention from the towpath. He had a bicycle, and
had waited an hour in the hope of getting a photograph of
Wynford. I told Wynford, and with his abounding good nature
he left his lunch to appear in the side hatchway while the delighted
boy snapped. Five minutes later the same boy overtook us, nearly
in tears. He had omitted to turn his camera and had superimposed
the picture. Would Mr Vaughan Thomas...? He would. Again
he left his meal and the boy made no mistake.

Those who regard the Black Country as an area swarming like
a rabbit warren with a pallid population, should travel the canal
from Wednesfield to Old Birchills Wharf, Walsall. It is a pleasant
wide waterway bordered by scrub country on the left, with
hawthorn and gorse abundant. On the right is a No Man's Land
of dead tree stumps rising from grey cinder, with 'swags' in the
hollows caused by mining subsidence. In Cheshire, one county to
northward, similar small pools caused by salt-mining subsidence
are known as 'flashes'.

This expansive moribund earth fills the foreground while the

usual South Staffordshire jungle of chimney-stacks and power
stations rises in the background. Of human habitation there is
none. Here man seems to have won his battle with the soil,
rendering it sterile in the conquest. Though Walsall Power
Station was our goal, as often as not we were moving away from
it so much does the canal wind, but ultimately, after a spell taking
us determinedly in the opposite direction, we turned sharp right
at Sneyd Junction Bridge and headed for the cooling towers which
rose like gigantic bobbins across the desolation.

Soon we were in a built-up area again.. As NORMAN
CHAMBERLAIN approached a new school of the modern single-
storey type it was obvious that an entertainment was in progress
in the main hall. We attracted no attention from a rapt audience.
But rounding an angle we brought a line of five classrooms into
view. As we sounded our horn those classrooms erupted. Children
jumped up, ran to the windows, opened doors, waved and
shouted, and as we disappeared under Brick Kiln Bridge chaos still
prevailed.

Traffic was becoming abundant again on the canal, noteworthy
being two tugs each pulling four open boats loaded with slack. On
each boat was a brazier belching smoke round the head of the
helmsman. These were Fred's home waters. As the helmsman of
each passing boat drew level he would mutter a series of non-
commital "Helloes" to various of us sprawled along our 70-foot
length. But coming abreast of Fred at the tiller he would explode
in amazement "Blimey Fred. Wot yo doin' thair? Yo do' arf get
some jobs."

Leaving the power station on our right we tied up in Old
Birchills Wharf. There Ernie Thomas has a home ashore and a
home afloat, evidence that there is still some money in his 300
canal boats. I thought the green lawn and bright flowers of his
garden more attractive than the pastel green and cream of his
converted narrow boat which struck me as incongruous on canals.

Fred's son had safely brought in the tug DOT on which I admired
Fred's own painting on tiller, bucket, and doorways. The night's
broadcast was to come from the wharf where already there was a
good crowd assembled. Reluctantly I left the cruise here, sorry to

be leaving such good company as Audrey and Wynford. A week later, after I had sent him a copy of my story on the journey in the *Birmingham Weekly Post*, Wynford wrote his thanks to me "I turn up the relevant chapter in *Fleas, Flukes, and Cuckoos* and find that a host is defined as 'a kindly being who does not resent but rather assists the parasites who batten on him'. Audrey and I were the flukes. You were the kindly hosts."

CHAPTER THREE

I start my four journeys by water from
Birmingham to the sea in the reverse direction,
and travel with nine million cheese rations up the
'King's High Stream of Severn'.

Cardiff must be a law-abiding city. As we drove slowly through its fine main roads we just could not find a policeman to direct us to the docks. The Force had impinged on our journey from Birmingham, and we were still wondering how the mobile policeman outside Monmouth had solved his problem.

We had passed out of that pleasant town beneath the 13th century gateway which spans Monnow Bridge, closely pursued by two lumbering tractors carrying outsize army tanks. A mile or so on, a policeman on a motor-cycle waved us to the side of the road.

"Just for a minute, please," he explained. "There's a very wide load approaching."

"Too bad," we said, "because a couple of tanks are following us."

The policeman's load hove in sight, a gigantic cogwheel protruding from a trailer well over half the width of the road. Much though we should have liked to see its head-on clash with the tanks, there was a tide to catch, and we hurried on towards Cardiff feeling even more convinced of the service waterways can do the community in relieving the roads of some loads.

But Cardiff seemed to be without a police force. So we enquired of a bus inspector, and soon found ourselves involved with dockside railway lines and shunting engines, breathing the smell compounded of timber, resin, tar, coal-dust, and ships, which is the same in all the ports of the world.

Our rendezvous was with SEVERN INDUSTRY in Queen Alexandra's Dock at noon. By courtesy of the Docks & Inland Waterways Executive, John Turnbull and I were to travel on her

from Cardiff to Worcester with a shipload of cheese. Thus I
should do the first of my four half-cardinal journeys, and also
produce an illustrated 'centre-spread' in the *Birmingham Weekly
Post* on how the Midlands gets its cheese ration. But instead of
travelling from Birmingham to the sea, I was travelling in a
reverse direction.

We found Queen Alexandra's Dock.

"Where's SEVERN INDUSTRY?" I asked an official.

"She's lying up alongside the meat boat," he replied, indicating
some warehouses above which masts towered. "Saw her there this
morning."

There was no mistaking the meat boat from the carcases passing
from her, through the sheds to a fleet of lorries, refrigerator
vehicles, and other conveyances. She was the NORFOLK from New
Zealand, and round the water side of her, the side from which one
does not expect merchandise to be disgorged, were two tiny
vessels, dwarfed by her towering white hull. One appeared
nameless, but on the outermost I could read the name SEVERN
MERCHANT.

That was half the name we wanted. So I walked along the quay
and climbed the steep gangway leading aboard NORFOLK, explained
to a watchman that I had business with the vessel on her other
side, and went round to look down on SEVERN MERCHANT. I
recoiled in horror. The rope ladder stretching down the hull of
NORFOLK looked frightful. Grasping the rail firmly, I hailed the
men who were stowing crates of cheese in the hold of the nearer
boat, afraid that I should be told it was on SEVERN MERCHANT we
were to travel.

But they pointed across the dock to where SEVERN INDUSTRY,
with her lighter, lay at quayside level. Thank goodness, no moun-
taineering necessary to board her, and when the skipper, having
been disturbed from a nap, offered us the alternatives of sailing at
1 p.m. with him on SEVERN INDUSTRY and making a night passage
from Avonmouth to Sharpness, or waiting for the MERCHANT and
sailing next morning up the river by daylight, I preferred the night
trip.

We stowed our kit on SEVERN INDUSTRY and, with an hour to

spare, went in search of food and of the ocean-going tug TURMOIL, which was in the docks. TURMOIL will long be remembered for her part in the FLYING ENTERPRISE drama* of January 1952, and as we looked at her lying sturdy and steady, it was hard to imagine her cavortings in a gale in the Western Approaches when Mate Kenneth Dancey jumped from her side to join Captain Carlsen on the disabled FLYING ENTERPRISE.

We were back aboard SEVERN INDUSTRY in good time, and, with half an hour to spare, were chugging across the dock, our lighter SABRINA 6 tied alongside like a Siamese twin, to take up position to be first in the lock when it opened. It was a beautiful sunny May day, but away to the north over the unseen mountains, the father and mother of a thunderstorm was brewing in a huge atomic mushroom-shaped cloud. The dock was still unruffled by shipping. ANDREAS from the North Pacific coast was unloading timber, with spelter below it which would be loaded on to one of SEVERN INDUSTRY'S sister ships when the timber was moved. A Portuguese vessel was filling her holds with coal nearby.

SEVERN INDUSTRY is a motor vessel of 78 tons net displacement, and cargo-carrying capacity of 160 tons; 89 feet long, 19½ feet in beam, and with a maximum speed of 7½ knots when on her own without a lighter in tow. Her consumption is between four and five gallons of diesel oil an hour. Two more tons displacement would put her in the coaster class. As it is she cannot ply seaward of Swansea and Barnstaple Bay. She has a mast which carries a sail in rough weather, but normally does nothing more than support the derrick which is now used almost exclusively for moving the lifeboat off the hatch when she is loading. Built by Charles Hill &

---

*On December 27th, 1951, the US freighter FLYING ENTERPRISE (6,711 tons) left Hamburg for New York. One day out it encountered a hurricane in the Western Approaches and its hull split open. One person was drowned, and the ship was abandoned by all but its Captain, Kurt Carlsen. On the sixth day of his lonely ordeal, Carlsen was joined by Kenneth Dancey, mate of the Admiralty tug TURMOIL who leapt aboard in mountainous seas to help to attach a towing hawser. TURMOIL then started a 450-mile tow towards Falmouth but, only 45 miles from harbour, the tow parted. The two men jumped into the sea and were rescued, but the FLYING ENTERPRISE sank.

Sons Ltd. of Bristol in 1934, she is of shallow draught for river work, and in the words of Tom Hunt, mate and engineer, "She'll roll the milk out of your tea in a rough sea." Most to the point, she can correctly be termed a 'barge', no little thing to a writer whose natural inclinations to call a canal-boat a barge have to be kept down in the interests of accuracy.

She has a wheelhouse aft, and on the after deck three hatchways lead, one to the engine room, the others to the crew's quarters, two cabins below decks, each with an upper and a lower berth. Forward on the port side is the W.C., an ordinary porcelain pedestal, flushed by water drawn up from sea, river, or canal, in a bucket with rope attached to the handle. Woe betide the unwary who drop the bucket overside thoughtlessly when the vessel is travelling at speed — there is a pull as it fills sufficient to jerk a man over the flimsy rail.

The lighter, named with the classical name of the river Severn — SABRINA 6 — had a wheelhouse aft, but was without a rail. On the tarpaulin stretched and secured over her hatch covers was a lifeboat with a bicycle propped against it. A variety of ropes lay neatly coiled on her deck, the thickest for towing in tidal waters, a thinner towing rope for the Gloucester & Berkeley Canal, and others for tying up to wharfs and piers.

SEVERN INDUSTRY had 1500 crates of cheese, close on 130 tons, while SABRINA 6 had a like amount. It had taken Cardiff dockers four hours to load SEVERN INDUSTRY on the previous afternoon, Sunday, and during the day they had filled two other barges and half-filled another, all from NORFOLK.

SEVERN INDUSTRY and her three SEVERN sister-ships, MERCHANT, STREAM, and TRADER, are now operated by British Waterways, of which the South-Western Division covers the area of the upper Bristol Channel ports, the Severn Valley, and the industrial areas of Birmingham and the Black Country. The Division is subdivided into two Districts, the Severn and the Midland, and the former, on which these vessels ply, covers the broad waterways centred on the River Severn between Avonmouth and Stourport. It also includes, though we are not concerned with them, the waterways between Bristol and Reading.

British Waterways took over these four vessels from the Severn
Carrying Company Ltd. under the terms of the Transport Act of
1947. Two hundred years ago, in 1752, Samuel Danks was born.
He founded a company under the name of S.Danks & Co. which
traded on the Severn and along the South Wales coast. He died in
1806, and the business was carried on by his sons and grand-
children under several names until 1873, when it was incorporated
as The Severn & Canal Carrying Shipping & Steam Towing Co.
Ltd. It is not surprising that it took two steps, half a century apart,
in 1891 and 1942, to abbreviate this unwieldy title to the Severn
Carrying Company Limited.

While we waited in the sunshine to enter the lock, Tom Hunt
told me of his sea-going career, and emphasised that in a south-
wester SEVERN INDUSTRY on the Bristol Channel is very much 'sea-
going'. Eighteen years in the Royal Navy had seen him in South
Africa, on the China Station, and with the Home Fleet. During
the war he served aboard RENOWN and ZAMBESI. Then followed a
spell ashore — at Swindon gasworks, but the feel of a deck beneath
his feet was an irresistible call which he managed to answer while
still not going too far or too long from home, by joining the
Severn Carrying Co. on April 9th, 1947. For eight months he was
aboard SEVERN VOYAGER, and with 3½ years on SEVERN INDUSTRY
he was the longest-serving of her crew.

Aboard SEVERN VOYAGER his usual routine had been two trips
weekly between Avonmouth and Stourport. SEVERN INDUSTRY
does at least one round journey each week between a Bristol
Channel port and Worcester or Stourport. From Avonmouth her
cargo is usually metal. Cheese, butter, tinned fruit and fish, and
metal are the cargoes mostly carried from Cardiff, Barry, or
Newport. By way of a change she sometimes plies from
Avonmouth to Bridgewater with woodpulp for the British
Cellophane Works, and we were later to see HALVARD BRATT of
Gotenburg, a Swedish vessel which brings woodpulp to Bristol
and Avonmouth.

While I was learning these things, SEVERN INDUSTRY had been
allowed in the lock, and we had taken up a good position at the sea
end as other vessels joined us. When the lock was full of shipping,

the inward gate was closed and sluices opened to lower our water
level to that of the sea outside. This necessitated about a 20-foot
drop down the glistening walls until the levels were equalised —
at low tide the drop would have been nearer forty feet.

Then the gates were opened, and as though a theatre curtain had
risen we were confronted by a new scene — a wooded promontory
to westward, and an oily flat calm merging with a haze through
which Flatholm could be seen but faintly, with Steepholm a vague
wraith beyond. A most formally named Dutchman, MR LINTHORST
HOMAN of Groningen, won the scramble to be first out, followed
by the tug LOYAL BRITON. As we took third place we dropped our
lighter astern, the tow rope gradually became taut, shook off a
shower of glistening drops, and we headed E.N.E. up Channel for
the English and Welsh Grounds Lightship. Behind us, also ran,
were NORA, MARGARET HAM, STANDARD ROSE, ERNEST BROWN and
several other craft. Fanning out, most went seaward, some sailed
up river.

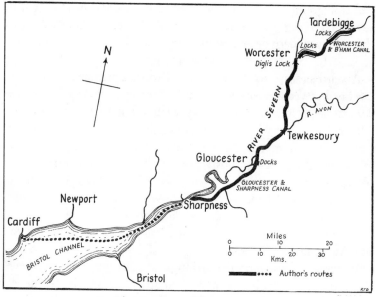

5: The Severn and its connections

Skipper Leslie Morgan, aged 31, at the wheel in the enclosed wheelhouse, looked little like a seaman in grey flannels, blue pullover, and striped shirt with open neck. Indeed, the only sartorial concession to the sea aboard was the glossy-peaked cap worn by Tom. A Gloucestershire man, from Dursley, the skipper had been with SEVERN INDUSTRY only three months, prior to which he was skipper of her sister ship SEVERN TRADER for four years. Joining the Severn Carrying Company as third hand at the age of 19, he became engineer after only nine months afloat.

I was allowed to take the wheel, which I did with some confidence born of my experience at the tiller of a canal boat. Surely a wheel would be easier. My mark on which to steer was the lightship, serene and steady, equidistant between the mast and a sheet.

"Keep her there and you'll be all right," I was told.

It was easier said than done. Remorselessly the lightship slid across our bows to the port side. I tugged at the wheel and made matters worse — she was now slipping rapidly along the horizon to port as our nose swung first towards the hazy Somerset coast and then in the direction of the open sea. Loud and rude comments came from Messrs Kingscote and May on the lighter as she tried to accommodate herself to our crazy course.

By herculean efforts I arrested our merry-go-round to starboard, and the lightship slowly crept back into the triangle between mast, sheet, and horizon where she had been originally. But there she would not stay, and this time went gambolling away along our starboard rail, while SEVERN INDUSTRY took a course towards the white chimney stack of Newport Power Station.

I was glad to surrender that wheel to the skipper, who told me that the weight of water on her helm makes her awkward, but that the lighter helps steady her.

Passing the lightship, and back again on a straight course, we chugged along a channel one mile wide between buoys, which brought us close to passing shipping. Colliers DOWNLEAZE and ROCKLEAZE had cargoes of coal from Cardiff to Portishead Power Station. Barges from Bristol were bound to Newport, also for coal. Off Portishead Nautical School we passed two Dutch motor-vessels — apparently the Dutch flag is increasingly seen in the Severn estuary. Next came two sand-suckers, DUNKERTON and SALTOM. We could see a stream of sand pouring into SALTOM's holds from a pipe trailed overboard — sand for the building industry in Bristol. And as the gleaming white warehouses of Avonmouth loomed ahead, a dredger wallowed out to drop her load in midstream.

Third hand Harry Parry of Newnham appeared with mugs of tea somewhere here. He had been a builder and a locomotive fireman before embracing the Severn in the wake of his father who had worked aboard one of three 'dumb barges' named after birds, SEVERN EAGLE, SEVERN HAWK, and SEVERN FALCON.

Slowly we nosed in beneath the shadow of a wooden jetty at Avonmouth and dropped our towline. SABRINA 6 drifted alongside again and tied up with us. Two balls slung from a mast at the lock-gate caused some bad language from our crew — they apparently excluded us from the lock — and there was no relenting when we blew four sharp blasts. So, with a portable wireless on deck, we lounged in the sunshine, though thunder grumbled almost incessantly up river.

"If we'd been going into Barry, Newport, or Cardiff, we'd have locked in, tied up, gone ahsore, and been bloody drunk by now," said the mate when we had waited nearly an hour.

Martin Kingscote and Jim May, the lighter's crew, had clambered on to the jetty to return with several pigeons' eggs, which can always be found in crannies among the piles. Martin came of a family of rivermen. His father was captain of the sailing barge SEVERN which plied from the Bristol Channel and Severn ports, his grandfather had also been a Severn skipper, his sister was a boatman's wife usually on the run between Sharpness and the Midlands, while he had two nephews on the Harker petrol barges whose acquaintance we were about to make. He had himself been 26 years with the Severn Carrying Company as mate. His lighter companion Jim May lived, like Martin, at Gloucester, and he could not shake off the Severn even in his own home, near Westgate Bridge where, in February 1947, he had six feet three inches of water in the house.

While we chatted, a barge with wheelhouse astern, not unlike SEVERN INDUSTRY, had drifted quietly against a jetty across the harbour mouth. A red flag with a white ball in the middle, proclaimed her inflammable cargo. She was WASTDALE H, one of the fleet of petroleum barges belonging to John Harker & Co. Ltd. which takes cargoes of petroleum from Avonmouth — where it is discharged by ocean-going tankers — to storage tanks at Gloucester, Worcester and Stourport.

I had nearly done my Severn trip aboard WASTDALE H in September 1951. Having applied to the owners for permission, which was granted, I was within one day of travelling to join her when the great fire occurred among the petroleum tanks at Avonmouth. Had this come two days later it might have given me the eye-witness story of a lifetime.* As it was, it prevented my making the journey at all — no bad thing, because SEVERN INDUSTRY's course and career were more interesting.

Ultimately the seaward lock gate opened and we followed WASTDALE H in, to be joined by two more of her tribe, WHARFEDALE H and HUNTDALE H, a Regent Petrol and Oil Company's tanker REGENT LADY, SEVERN VOYAGER, and SEVERN ROVER.

"Where you from? What cargo?" shouted a uniformed figure on the waterside.

We told him, the water level rose in the lock, the gate opened, and we chugged slowly across a basin surrounded by cranes and derricks to our berth. It was 7 p.m. and we were waiting for a tide at 1.30 a.m. Skipper, mate, third hand, and John were tidying up for a pub-crawl — Jim hadn't even worried to tidy up. Martin, in less of a hurry, watched more shipping coming up the lock and seemed to know every boat intimately. SUNRISEN was a diesel boat running regularly to Worcester with wheat for Townshend's Albion Flour Mill.

---

*Even more dramatic than the Avonmouth fire was WASTDALE's eventual end. On October 25th, 1960, WASTDALE H and ARKENDALE H missed the entrance to Sharpness Lock in the fog. While attempting to get back to the entrance, they collided and then hit the Severn Railway Bridge. The collapse of the bridge caused the two boats to explode, killing five of the eight crew. The bridge was beyond repair, and was eventually dismantled in 1968.

There was a distant hoot from an unseen ship away on the river. "That's IRIS, a steam tug," said Martin, and sure enough in fifteen minutes or so IRIS appeared from the lock with a train of boats in tow.

"SEVERN EAGLE, CHEDWORTH, SEVERN CONVEYOR," Martin told me with the merest glance, and so they were as their names approached close enough to be read. A white ocean-going vessel BEN NEVIS was disgorging timber within 200 yards of us, and astern of her was CRUX of Bergen.

When Martin followed the others ashore I was left sole custodian of nine million cheese rations. This was my chance of some sleep — I anticipated none during the night. So, taking a last look at the evil sky up river, a bronze glow above a pall of black from which incessant thunder growled and lightning flashed, I went below and lay on the skipper's bunk.

But the cabin was uncomfortably hot and the approaching storm irresistible, so I went on deck again to watch the lightning and its reflection in the glassy water, until a sharp shower drove me below to stay.

The noise which awoke me was much more fearsome than thunder — our engine starting up within a few feet of my ears through the bulkhead. It was 1.15 a.m. and the returning revellers had not awakened me. The rain was finished and the sky starlit. Tom was perambulating the deck with the port and starboard lights, and the dock basin was strangely beautiful, black arms of cranes against a glow of white lights, spears of white and orange reflected in the oily water.

Then a black shape stole across the basin, and the spears buckled and danced as a tanker, bearing down on the lock, ruffled the water. The dock was coming to life. Other tankers glided down from the storage tanks, WASTDALE H much lower in the water with 300 tons of petroleum in her holds. Each of them bore a red light above their white mast-head light, the after dark equivalent of the 'inflammable' flag.

The lock side had awakened too. Three white-capped figures were busying themselves up there as we went steadily down, some 25 feet or so. Two tugs, PLUMSGARTH and KINGSGARTH, had joined us. SEVERN VOYAGER with the favoured centre position as the great gates swung open was out before others of us had started. Then, like greyhounds from the slips, we all followed her into the night.

Because we had our lighter in tow we soon fell behind the petrol barges. Their red lights were visible from astern, and through them, bobbing ahead, the skipper was searching for a fast blinking white light — colloquially a 'quick-flasher', — which he then tried to get to the left of a 'slow-flasher'. These were Redcliff and Charston lights respectively. I stood in the wheelhouse, fascinated by this night navigation. I had been sorry to miss a daytime passage of the estuary, but this was ample compensation.

We were in the dark. The skipper bent over occasionally and, drawing hard at his cigarette, peered at the compass in the glow. Now and then he turned to look through the rear windows at SABRINA 6 swinging slightly on her tow rope and showing red and green alternately. Once he pointed out a cluster of lights from the pumping station which pumps water out of the Severn railway tunnel. Completed in 1886, the tunnel, which links Bristol and Newport, is 4 miles 624 yards long — 2¼ miles of its length running beneath the river itself.

About 40 minutes out we were near Charston light, and chasing another will-o-the-wisp, a 'green-flasher', Chapel Light, off Beachley where Wye enters Severn below Chepstow. As we approached Chapel Light its green flashes turned to white — our clue to veer somewhat towards it.

We had a glimpse of Aust cliffs, Somerset terminus of the car and passenger ferry from Beachley, to starboard, and then seemed to stand well in under Sedbury Cliffs on the northern shore. Somewhere up there Offa's Dyke set off on its northern march of 140 miles along the Welsh border. Four years earlier, after copious reading about the Dyke, I sought its beginning on those cliffs, to walk along its length. And in the moment of first finding it, the discovery meant nothing to me beside the pink stars of centaury studding the cliff-top. I am botanist long before I am antiquarian.

When it seemed to me that we were bent on running ashore beneath a huge wall of cliff which loomed in the darkness ahead, the skipper turned the wheel and SEVERN INDUSTRY sheered off to starboard across the river. As we were now running against wind and tide, instructions were shouted down to Harry to shut the portholes. And now I witnessed another intricacy of estuarial navigation by night. As though it was not enough having to keep his eyes skinned for'ard, the skipper now had to steer by lights astern, getting the two Inward Rocks Lights in line behind us, and aiming at Counts Lights on the other shore.

By 4 a.m. black was turning to grey and I still kept my bleary-eyed vigil in the wheelhouse where Tom and Harry had joined us to make the night hideous with song. Sharpness Light could be seen ahead, nodding across the river to a light at Lydney, and through the glasses I could pick out a train on the northern shore on its journey towards South Wales. We were now well in towards the southern shore.

The skipper had remarked during the night on the exceptional clarity of the lights, fearing that it portended wind or rain, and as dawn became more pronounced all the signs bore out his dreary prediction. Through the grey light we could now see a fair-sized Greek ship aground on Lydney Sands where she stuck when her tow-rope parted at Easter 1951 as she was carrying a cargo of maize into Sharpness.

A flotilla of empty petroleum tankers passed us some way out of Sharpness, sailing down river on the morning tide. But a red light shone against us on a mast at the lock, and with much vilification of the Sharpness authorities, the skipper and Tom bent to the considerable job of holding SEVERN INDUSTRY off the jetty against a murky current which was racing up river at about four knots, and they felt thankful that it was not the big 30-foot tide which rattles past at seven knots. Severn tides are the biggest in Europe.

It was getting lighter every minute. What I had taken to be two very symmetrical domed hills upstream resolved themselves into two arches of the Severn Bridge. The cliffs flanking Lydney changed from black to chocolate. A strong smell of hawthorn was wafted offshore, reminding me of a passage of the Kiel Canal in the May before war broke out in 1939, when along its whole length the air was redolent with lilac. There is a shipboard smell, unvarying whatever the ship, and even our cheese had not made itself manifest over that of SEVERN INDUSTRY. But the occasional land smell prevails.

South Gloucestershire is a famous countryside for elms, and we amused ourselves during a weary wait by finding strange silhouettes among them. One tableau was a perfect representation of two girls embracing; the one on the left with hair below her shoulders; the right a rather skinny type with a bustle. Even the arms and shoulders stretched between them were there.

As a rosy flush drew our attention to a huge watery pink sun with stratified clouds across it, we were joined by a tug towing SEVERN FALCON, with cocoa beans from Avonmouth, and by a petroleum barge. When, from time to time, we slipped back a little with the running tide, we could see round a corner of the jetty a shipbuilding yard, where at a slipway on a grassy bank SEVERN TIDE was being built — twice the size of SEVERN INDUSTRY.

Just as Tom was remarking that Sharpness should be renamed Slowness the lock gate opened to give exit to the tug STANEGARTH, identified by a cockerel on her mast. She had two barges in tow and was followed by more of the ubiquitous petroleum barges. That confounded red light was extinguished, a ball dropped down the mast, and we locked in at 6 a.m., rising to the basin, and changing our lighter's tow from the heavy sea rope to the slimmer one for the canal. Our mast had been lowered as there were bridges to negotiate on our next lap — the Gloucester & Berkeley Canal.

The Severn between Sharpness and Gloucester is circuitous and hazardous, though by expert use of canvas and tide the old sailing 'trows' could make the passage from Bristol to Gloucester in 24 hours. When in the latter half of the 18th century the new canals of the Midlands, and the east to west routes such as the Thames & Severn Canal from the Stroudwater Navigation near Stroud to the Thames near Lechlade, were bringing more trade to the river, the value of safe and speedy communication with the sea was obvious. So a ship canal was proposed from Gloucester to Berkeley Pill, 18¼ miles away on the estuary. (Pill means inlet, and is common in these parts.) An authorizing Act was passed on March 28th, 1793, but not until 1827 was traffic passing over England's first ship canal. Its completion differed from its conception. Although the name has remained, the southern outlet was changed from Berkeley Pill to Sharpness Point, thus reducing the canal's length to 16½ miles. When, in 1874, a bigger entrance lock and a new dock were opened at Sharpness, the company took the name of the Sharpness New Docks and Gloucester & Birmingham Navigation Company.

Today, vessels with cargo capacity of up to 9000 tons can be docked and discharged at Sharpness. We saw SUPREMITY off Severn Mills, LEITRIM, a grain sucker, and TOUJOURS PRET, and in places the docks are lined with wartime concrete barges used now for storage.

Chugging into the canal, SEVERN INDUSTRY left the old entrance to port with a Merchant Navy training ship down it, and passed under Severn Bridge, opened in 1879, which carried the railway to the Forest of Dean. There are 22 spans, and some estimate of the tortuous nature of the river can be gained with the knowledge that the navigable channel runs only through the two northernmost spans.*

For a short distance the canal runs above and parallel with the river, only a few yards of hawthorn-crowned embankment separating the two. On the other hand — our right (port and starboard should be discarded on the canal) were reedy meres populous with swans and herons.

The limit on the canal is five m.p.h. with a £20 fine on masters exceeding it. Slowly we came up to our first bridge where we had to wait for our bridgeman or passman. He soon arrived on a bicycle and turned a windlass to open the bridge. Meanwhile a herd of cows meandered leisurely across another bridge 100 yards ahead as we admired the creeper-clad Berkeley Hunt Inn.

A number of graceful white wooden swing bridges span the canal. The width of the channel being 70 feet, these bridges are in two portions, opening from the centre. At each a bridge-keeper, resident in a spectacular little lodge with cream portico supported on two brown fluted pillars, opens one side, while that on the opposite bank is opened by the passman who accompanies a boat

---

* see footnote on page 59 for an account of the fate of this bridge.

1: The author at the tiller of NORMAN CHAMBERLAIN

2: Sir Frank Nelson aboard DULCE DOMUM

3: Preparing for bed aboard NORMAN CHAMBERLAIN

4: Thomas Clayton's base at Junction Wharf, Oldbury

5: Limestone formation inside Dudley Tunnel

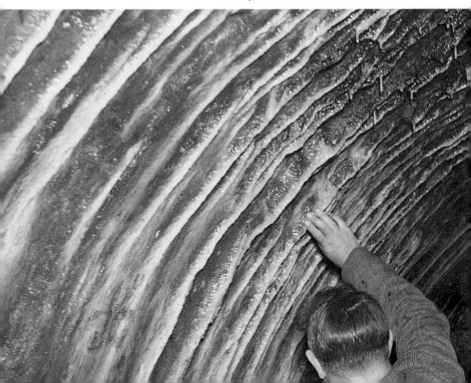

6: Near Bumble Hole, on B.B.C. cruise. Wynford Vaughan Thomas
is talking to the photographer near the bow

7: Paul Winterforde-Young and Wynford Vaughan Thomas (seated)
approaching Netherton Tunnel

8: Southern end of Netherton Tunnel

9: SEVERN INDUSTRY leaving Cardiff Docks

10: Peter Scott's BEATRICE at Slimbridge

11: SEVERN INDUSTRY at Tewkesbury, 1952 (© National Waterways Museum)

12: The Boat & Railway Inn, Stoke Works, near Bromsgrove

13: Typical lock cottage on the Stratford-on-Avon Canal

on his bicycle from Berkeley Hunt Inn to Hempsted Bridge, Gloucester, a pleasant enough job in fine weather, but the very devil in rain such as now greeted us.

Rain-rings intersected with fish-rings in the water as we pursued our rural way. Comfrey was the commonest flower on the banks, purple and cream, and teazels grew in the ditches. Sometimes the east bank was fringed with willows while a towpath followed the other with its solitary cyclist dripping wetter and wetter, but unflaggingly opening bridges before us and closing them as we passed through.

When we drew level with the slim spire of Slimbridge church, we passed the converted narrow boat BEATRICE, moored alongside 'The Patch' Guest House.* BEATRICE is the property of the Severn Wildfowl Trust, whose New Grounds are on the river a mile away. Wild duck from the Trust can often be seen winging their rapid flight across the canal, for there are three types of bird in the pens — the 'full-winged' which have normal power of flight but having been hand-reared on the Grounds do not stray; the 'feather-cut' with flight feathers of one wing cut to prevent flying temporarily until new flight feathers are grown after moulting; and the 'pinioned' birds, permanently grounded, with the tip of the wing bone, which bears the flight feather, cut when young.

BEATRICE was used as a floating hostel for students who wished to study birds on the spot, but proved an unsuccessful venture.

Soon after, an old canal ran off to the right towards the village of Cambridge on the Bristol road. We had scarcely passed the attractive little cottage in a flower-decked garden at its junction than we were passing the village of Frampton, pleasantly thatched, on our right, its war memorial cross plainly seen from the canal. Tom told me that the shadows of the old sailing ships used to fall on Frampton church tower many years ago, and certainly it is only a stone's throw from the church porch to the canal.

---

*BEATRICE was converted (in the same style as Tom Rolt's CRESSY) for Peter Scott, the IWA's first Vice-President. Scott used the boat on some of the IWA's early campaign cruises, during one of which the GWR were obliged to lift a bridge they had fixed over the Stratford Canal, impeding navigation.

There was always some feature of interest to punctuate our
rainy journey. A houseboat of punt-like design had a grindstone
and was piled with stakes for work on the banks. Then we were
passing Cadbury's factory on the right with the trees of Fretherne
Court facing it across our course. There had been a glimpse of the
river from Frampton before it curved away around an isthmus on
the neck of which we caught a sight of Saul Church through the
trees.

A row of white hulls of cabin cruisers seen across a meadow on
the right proved to be moored on the Stroudwater Canal, a
waterway first authorised in 1730 to link Framilode on the Severn
with Stroud, but not completed until July 1779. At the junction
with the Sharpness Canal there is a boat yard where repairs are
done to wooden vessels, and from the number of cruisers in the
first hundred yards of the Stroudwater, the business should be
thriving.

Near the Pilot Inn was a barge for bank works, and from it a
number of close-shorn heads peered out into the rain from which
they were sheltering — prisoners of Gloucester Gaol in the charge
of a uniformed warder. At a sharp right turn near Stonebench,
canal and river are only a few hundred yards apart, but we saw no
sign of the Severn. Week-end shacks and bungalows were
beginning to line the Canal. At Lower Rea Bridge a children's
school bus was held up as we passed, a reminder of the surprising
fact that the time was not yet 9 a.m. though we seemed to have
packed a fair day's experience into the hours of daylight. We were
preceded through Upper Rea Bridge by a swan which took flight
at our approach, and hereabouts John came sleepily on deck having
slept almost since Avonmouth, missing many interesting subjects
for his camera.

The tower of Gloucester Cathedral could now be seen ahead,
and pickling ponds for timber led from the Canal. Gloucester's
industries had begun, and at Hempsted Bridge our drenched
passman left us. A notice warned 'Dead Slow For One Mile' and
we crept past the timber yards on our right so as not to break the
mooring ropes of barges lying there. More pickling ponds piled
with logs, and we were abreast of Monk Meadow where some of

the petroleum barges discharge their cargoes. A huge grain silo towered overhead, and at Llanthony Bridge, entrance to the docks, were more warehouses for cotton seed, linseed, and ground nuts. Coasting vessels carrying up to 700 tons can be handled at Gloucester.

We left SABRINA 6 at Gloucester to continue up to Worcester on the morrow with a tug. Without her, SEVERN INDUSTRY could have made the passage to Stourport by 4 p.m. Her record run was 19 hours from Cardiff to Stourport.

At Gloucester Mr H. A. Roberts, Severn District Traffic Officer of the Docks & Inland Waterways Executive turned out in the rain to greet us. Conversing from boat to lock-side as one locks down is a humorous business. You begin face to face with one another. Then gradually the boat falls and while you rise on your toes the man ashore does a steady knees bend to keep level. Then you slip below his boots and he retains his crouching position until it dawns upon him that it looks undignified, when he straightens up and raises his voice. You are now some 20 feet, maybe, below him.

I know no more beautiful city than Gloucester as seen from St. Catherine's Meadows alongside the Severn. The railway embankment serves it as a wall, behind which rises the majesty of the loveliest of English cathedrals with lesser towers and spires doing it reverence. Distant some ten miles is the rim of the Cotswolds. From my schooldays, whenever I read 'The Passing' by W.E. Henley, I thought of Gloucester

> '. ....from the west
> Where the sun, his day's work ended,
> Lingers as in content,
> There falls on the old, gray, city
> An influence luminous and serene,
> A shining peace.
>
> The smoke ascends
> In a rosy and golden haze. The spires
> Shine, and are changed...'

And how delighted I was to find, later, that Henley was a
Gloucester man, and that doubtless the city inspired his poem. For
was not my first poem written beside the Severn at Gloucester?

Sterner things than poetry confronted SEVERN INDUSTRY, and the
skipper was having a terrific wrestling match with the wheel on
the twists and turns of the river. We had forsaken the placid canal
for a fast-running current with quite a lot of 'fresh' in it, for the
rain was widespread and had become a downpour.

Floods raise problems for SEVERN INDUSTRY. Only a fortnight
earlier the river rose seven feet while she was up at Stourport, and
all the superstructure had to be taken down to get under the
bridges down river. The top half of the wheelhouse is removable,
as is the wheel itself, and even the closet on the forepeak is hinged,
and two feet or so can be taken off its height. With a good flood
which is not high enough to cause bridge trouble, SEVERN
INDUSTRY can travel from Stourport to Gloucester in three hours
instead of her normal six.

But on one occasion with nine feet of 'fresh' it took two hours
to pass beneath Gloucester railway bridge. The bridge was
approached stern first, that being the lower end, with as much
water ballast as possible. The stern having been wedged through,
the water was released, which brought it up and the forward end
down.

Fortunately we had no such problems to contend with, and the
twists safely negotiated, we had a good run up the wide straight
Long Reach from Maisemore Arm to Ashleworth, making our
own little Severn Bore which ran along the bank with us, playfully
lapping in the rat-holes. On this reach we passed a sandsucker.

The miniature beach below Wainlode Hill, Gloucester's lido on
a fine summer day, was empty, and wreaths of mist rose from the
trees to make a cap for the crest of the hill. Beyond the trees, the
hill rises bare and precipitous from the river, in strata of gray and
chocolate, broken in places by landslips. Some barges have been
sunk at Wainlode to prevent the current undercutting the bank of
the popular riverside field, and it was indicative of the 'fresh' that
we could not see them from the surface.

A stream enters the river at the upper end of Wainlode field, followed soon by the disused Coombe Hill Canal with a narrow lock holding its waters from those of the Severn.

A series of riverside inns brought us to Upper Lode Lock outside Tewkesbury — Haw Bridge Inn, The New Inn, White Lion Inn ('accommodation' spelt correctly, and a caravan site), Yew Tree Inn (with two yews and sand martins nesting in the banks nearby), and Lower Lode Hotel (opposite a boathouse with a 1947 flood mark plainly shown). There is a complicated river system at the waterlogged town of Tewkesbury. The Avon splits and has two confluences with the Severn, one at Lower Lode, the other two miles on, north of Severn Ham, Tewkesbury's expansive water-meadow. In between them the Severn itself breaks into three at Upper Lode where the lock takes vessels up the westernmost arm, past a substantial lock house bearing the date 1858.

As we cleared Tewkesbury at 1 p.m. — 24 hours out of Cardiff — the rain had ceased. We celebrated with our first serious meal — beans, bacon, and eggs — and set off in pursuit of HUNTDALE H which was nearly half a mile ahead. The alder was taking over from the willow as we travelled north, and our view was much more restricted than in the Canal — a spire rising mistily among trees, or a stately home in its grounds. Beyond the railway bridge at Saxon's Lode were jetties for storage tanks of aviation spirit for nearby aerodromes, and the intake for Coventry's water supply.

Upton, which has a 'White Swan' and a 'King's Head' visible from the river, is distinguished by a graceful spire and disgraced by a baroque dome. This monstrosity goes well enough up to a tower which is a mixture of reddish and greenish stone surmounted at the four corners by inapt urns. Then it runs riot in a helter-skelter-like top, piling one on top of another a mouldy green dome, an open-sided lookout, and a weather-vane.

On Upton's bridge a gull flew over a Midland Red bus, the sea we had left greeting the Midlands we were approaching. Seagulls were not uncommon, flying singly down river, deviating neither to left nor right. Once a kingfisher, fish in beak, flashed across the river with rapid clockwork wing beat, so different from the ponderous flapping of the heron which disappeared over the leafy ridge of some red cliffs, where fallen trees lay in tumbled confusion on our left.

We overtook M.B.BRIDGET, belonging to Charles Ballinger of Gloucester, carrying a cargo between Cadbury's Frampton factory and Bournville; and a little later PISGAH, a barge which usually runs up the Lower Avon navigation with grain for Pershore Mill. A dredger looked almost like a Mississippi showboat with its big smoke stack, and a narrow boat of the Midlands canals hauled its tow past us full of mud and sand.

Soon the River Teme joined the Severn from the west, its straight and canal-like channel so different from its Shropshire wanderings

'In valleys of springs of rivers,
    By Onny, and Teme, and Clun.'

Cabin cruisers and houseboats began to line our route, until, with Worcester's cathedral tower in sight, a slender spire to the left of its bulk, SEVERN INDUSTRY nosed into Diglis Lock. The date on the lock house is 1844, and there are up and down locks. Bill, plump and in a canary sweater, opened up for us, and we glided to the quay where, at 4 p.m. we said "Good-bye" to SEVERN INDUSTRY, which made off immediately for Stourport, fifteen more miles up river.

Diglis Quay is 320 feet long and 50 feet wide, allowing three barges of 150 tons each to be loaded or discharged simultaneously. The steel transit shed has a storage capacity of 190,000 cubic feet, and modern diesel cranes of two and five tons capacity transfer cargoes speedily from barge to transit shed or direct to road vehicle. In fact SEVERN STREAM which sailed a day earlier from Cardiff than SEVERN INDUSTRY, was discharging her cargo direct on to lorries for transport to a food store at Warwick. And here, on Diglis Quay, I had my first whiff of cheese since leaving Cardiff.

POSTSCRIPT, 1967

It was 1967 before I travelled the Worcester & Birmingham Canal northwards, one of a dozen canal journeys for a series of

articles in the *Sunday Mercury* including a delightful cruise on the
Irish Grand Canal, and one on the Leicester Canal which I thought
the loveliest of Midlands canals.

Hoping for a lift on the Worcester & Birmingham I asked the
lock-keeper at Diglis Basin, Dennis Merrell, if any boats had
passed through ahead of me, though it was only 8.45 a.m.

"LAUGHING WATER went up late yesterday," he told me. "You
might catch them, or ELFIN — a young man and his girl."

They wouldn't want an ageing gooseberry aboard, but
LAUGHING WATER offered possibilites. It might have moored overnight at Tibberton Locks six miles away and made a late start. So
off I strode up the unbeautiful cut through Worcester, behind the
Royal Porcelain Works and past an odoriferous yard full of
sheepskins, to take a short cut along Tolladine Road, saving a mile
with the chance of a hitch.

Back on the canal I saw no boats, nor had some fishermen. This
apart it was a good wide towpath through Tibberton — and for
the entire 17 miles to Tardebigge. The Worcester & Birmingham
is as tough as any in Britain, with 58 locks in those 17 miles, and
three tunnels and intricate bends between Tardebigge and Gas
Street, Birmingham. The strategy of catching a boat uphill was to
get it on the six Tibberton Locks and cruise comfortably along the
5½-miles pound to the next locks at Dodderhill, but I had failed.
With Tibberton behind them, any boats ahead would be gaining
on me. So I settled down to another 12 miles.

At Oddingley the canal runs alongside the railway, a perfect
picture of rural peace seen from the train, grey canal bridge,
timbered farmhouse, tall elms, and a country church — but its
story was far from peaceful. There in 1806 one Richard
Hemming, a Droitwich wheelwright, was commissioned to shoot
the rector by five landowners who objected to paying tithes.
Having done so Hemming hid in Trench Wood nearby and
became an embarrassment to his backers, who lured him down to
Netherwood Farm and murdered him, burying him beneath a
barn. There he lay until 1830 when his remains were unearthed as
the barn was demolished. The barn built in its place has in its outer
wall a stone inscribed '1806 R.H.1830. R.I.P.' The railway

embankment on my right blotted out Netherwood Farm but left a view along the skyline of Trench Wood, a glorious place for flowers in spring and nightingales in July.

Passing Fir Tree Inn I came to Dunhampstead's 236-yards tunnel which I skirted via Tunnel House Farm, and passing through Shernal Green, where trim cottages have flower beds and well-cut lawns on the canal bank, I came to the marina at Hanbury Wharf. I had walked 10 miles from Worcester. The 'Eagle & Sun' of the inn sign at Hanbury is the crest of the Galton family, once of nearby Hadzor. Of the several boats moored opposite the pub none was pointing my way, but when I hailed the male occupant of a cabin cruiser, the GILMAN KEVEN, he said he was turning back towards Tardebigge and would welcome me aboard. So I joined Arthur Humphries of Harborne, Birmingham, who told me that the boat was once a seaplane tender and did several trips to Dunkirk to bring off troops during the 1940 evacuation. So, even if you are not a messer-about-in-boats, look with respect on the strange assortment of craft that ply our canals.

There was no lazing for me. I had got my lift too late. In 1½ miles we were climbing up the Dodderhill Five, and I was lending a hand in that most perilous of occupations: raising the lock paddles. But journey's end was in sight, with Tardebigge's needle spire visible in the north. Stoke Works brought industry to the waterside with memories of busy canal days from John Corbett's salt works when the Droitwich Junction arm, now derelict, linked the Worcester Canal at Hanbury with the Droitwich Canal in its lovely 6-mile course to the Severn at Hawford Lock.

Trade practically ended on the Worcester & Birmingham Canal with the death in 1962 of Charlie Ballinger, a famous Number One, whose narrow boats, OLIVE and ENERGY among them, carried chocolate crumb between Bournville and Cadbury's Works at Frampton-on-Severn. Recently, though, 'Sam' Waller's Birmingham & Midland Canal Carrying Company had brought timber by narrow boat from Sharpness up the Worcester & Birmingham to King's Norton and down the Stratford and the Grand Union to Warwick.

Our wash swept against the walls of canalside cottages at Stoke

Works, and glasses were raised to us by workers enjoying their pints in the verandah of the Boat & Railway Inn. When the GILMAN KEVEN stopped for lunch at Stoke Wharf I walked on. Tied up there with other boats was the old Fellows, Morton & Clayton 'josher' LYNX, belonging to my friend Keith Christie. Built in 1913 it was one of a small class of narrow boats fitted with Bollinder engines, and to Keith it was a working boat.

Beyond Stoke Works I was ascending Tardebigge's fearsome 30 locks. Ten locks up I overtook LAUGHING WATER and introduced myself to Jack Tompkins who was at the wheel while his son and daughter locked ahead and his wife opened and closed the upper gates. They were returning to their Stratford home after cruising to Upton-on-Severn. So well-drilled a team were they that I felt less compunction at becoming a complete parasite as I sat and chatted to Mr Tompkins while LAUGHING WATER steadily rose up the locks. When I learned that he is the Deputy Chairman of the Upper Avon Navigation Trust I understood the boatmanlike qualities of his family. LAUGHING WATER is a 48½-foot Thames launch. I asked when he had acquired her.

"Let me see," he mused, "in that good wine year, 1959." Her original owner, Lady Astor, the redoubtable teetotal M.P. wouldn't have liked that, nor perhaps the fact that two brewers have owned the launch since her day. Her aristocratic connections are not LAUGHING WATER's sole claim to fame. She was the first boat to navigate the southern section of the Stratford Canal before the official re-opening by the Queen Mother, and at the celebration rally of boats at Stratford in July 1964 a stray Jack Russell terrier walked aboard. He is still with them — Charlie.

"But for Charlie you wouldn't have caught us," said Mr Tompkins as we reached my hard-won destination, Tardebigge, at 5 p.m. "He chased two goats down the canal and it took us some time to round them up."

CHAPTER FOUR

*In which I take to the towpath for a change,
and, on the southern section of the Stratford-on-
Avon Canal find Arcadia in Arden.*

My canal wanderings for 1953 began on a bitter Monday in
February, I had spent the week-end at Nash Court, the Shropshire
training centre of the National Association of Boys' Clubs, to
write a story about a treasure hunt on the Clee Hills. This had been
pursued in a snowstorm, adding considerable piquancy to a nine
mile cross-country journey in broken country, which introduced
me to one of the loveliest villages I have ever seen, Hope Bagot,
nestling at the foot of a wooded Devon-like combe — an all-too-
fleeting acquaintance, as I slithered into it with seven boys and a
sledge, followed up certain clues round a Norman font in the
delightful church, and panted out up a steep field where molehills
frozen hard as rocks rendered the manhandling of a sledge laden
with a tent no easy matter.

When I dodged away from Nash by car after tea, snow was still
falling and it seemed possible that the boys would be marooned for
the night, the coach from Birmingham unable to reach them. So
next morning I rang Paul to enquire their ultimate fate and was
told that they made their getaway and reached Birmingham safely,
but that the boys spending the week-end aboard NORMAN
CHAMBERLAIN had not been so lucky. Ice had delayed their return
from Tardebigge, and on Sunday night they had abandoned ship,
leaving her stuck solid at Cobley. Word had just come of an ice-
breaker going through, so Paul's henchman, Jim Thomas, and
Sheila from the Federation office, were setting out to try to bring
the boat back to its basin at King's Norton.

I joined them, and we were driven to Cobley, but the canal
showed no signs of an ice-breaker having passed. We trudged in
deep snow along the towing-path to where NORMAN CHAMBERLAIN

lay at her usual moorings, and took stock of the situation. It appeared that attempts had been made the previous evening to continue towards Birmingham, for in mid-canal there was a channel about 200 yards long of ice only one night thick, fringed by a seemingly impenetrable white border. We started her up, and with much shafting put her nose at the thinner ice. I stood on the forepeak clouting the ice with the long pole, and very slowly we advanced into the cracks produced by my Herculean efforts.

In half-an-hour we had successfully accomplished the 200 yards of the channel and were at grips with the thicker stuff. My assault with the hooked shaft barely scratched the surface, and we were in midstream ramming away abortively when a boys' club leader hove in sight on the towpath. Having a car at the bridge, he volunteered to fetch us some food, and to phone the Inland Waterways people and enquire about an ice-breaker. He returned with bacon and eggs which we dragged aboard over the ice in a bucket on the boat-hook, and not much later the ice-breaker chugged unconcernedly through, leaving behind a boat-wide channel to King's Norton.

Thereafter it was easier than steering in normal conditions. The weight of ice on either side corrected any tendency to edge in to the mud, and we accomplished the journey in excellent time, drifting for a while in the cutting before Wast Hill Tunnel at dusk while we ate a memorable meal prepared by Sheila. Since my last chapters I had spent one September week-end on NORMAN CHAMBERLAIN, and our outward passage of Wast Hill Tunnel had been marked by a momentary encounter near the half-way vent with a heroic character paddling through in a rubber dinghy. I was in the bows and saw his torch low on the water beyond the rays of our searchlight. The height of a light above water level can be judged in a tunnel by the distance between it and its reflection, and in this case that was practically nil. I realised it must be a canoe or some such craft, so shouting to our helmsman to slow down, I bawled through the megaphone that we had seen the other approaching, and watched him materialise in our searchlight's beam, draw level, and swirl down our side to disappear astern.

With the Spring of 1953 came the desire to be out and about on canals again. The one-inch Ordnance map, that most fruitful ground for the journalist in search of a subject, gave me my serious introduction to the Stratford-on-Avon Canal, curling its slim blue length half over my Birmingham sheet, the other half over the Stratford sheet, and I resolved to travel it afoot.

Conveniently it falls into two equal halves; some 13 miles to the north and 13 to the south of Kingswood, where not only is the canal depot situated, but there is also a junction with the Grand Union — the main canal from Birmingham to London. L.T.C. Rolt, that doyen of canal historians, was worried lest the Stratford Canal become impassable before he could realise the dream of a narrow boat of his own. However, the northern section is still navigable from the Grand Union at Kingswood to its junction at King's Norton with the Worcester & Birmingham Canal, and I believe Mr Rolt's CRESSY has made the passage.

Whatever may be the fate of the Stratford Canal, it has its place

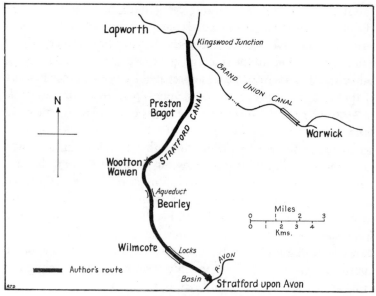

6: The Stratford-on-Avon Canal

in literature. That garrulous George Borrow of the waterways, E. Temple Thurston, pursuing his way and his conversation by a circular route from and back to Oxford, travelled the southern section in the FLOWER OF GLOSTER and sang its praises. And Quiller-Couch, far from his Cornish coasts, wrote a novel *True Tilda* in which a narrow boat SUCCESS TO COMMERCE cleaves the arrow-head and other aquatic flora on this canal.

The Act of Parliament was granted in 1793, and work began at King's Norton, the northern end. Those were the days when canals were jealous of their water, and 200 yards from the junction with the Worcester Canal, a guillotine lock was constructed to prevent the flow of water from the one canal into the other. Unused since nationalisation brought the waterways under one management, the lock still remains, open but in perfect preservation — a rare relic. It consists of two guillotines a good boat's length apart, which were raised and lowered in slots by winches. Normally these were kept lowered. On the approach of a boat from the Worcester Canal, the nearer guillotine was raised and the boat passed beneath it into the lock, the guillotine being lowered behind it. The far one was then raised, to be lowered after the boat was hauled out of the lock into the Stratford Canal. Thus neither side had lost water. As Lifford Lane bridge spans the canal between the two guillotines, with the lock house standing by, a most impressive assemblage of canal architecture results.

By 1798 half the distance had been cut, and the canal was open to Hockley Heath. Five more years elapsed with progress still no farther than Lapworth and the Company's funds exhausted. In 1808, £2000 was advanced by the Stratford Corporation, which saw the commercial advantage of a water link in the town with the Avon, and work went forward 1¼ miles beyond the aqueduct across the main road at Wootton Wawen. Through efforts of William James, the Henley-in-Arden engineer, the canal was ultimately completed, and opened on June 24th, 1816.

It attracted considerable traffic, but in 1857 met the fate of many canals — it was bought up by one of their new competitors, the railways — the Oxford, Worcester & Wolverhampton. This became part of the Great Western Railway, whose boundary posts still stud the canal banks, and the canal is now managed by the Docks & Inland Waterways Executive.

My world was as dew-pearl'd as that of Robert Browning's optimistic jingle, though it was an hour later, when I joined the Stratford Canal at Kingswood on the first Sunday in May, a morning which already gave promise of a day which was to set up sunshine records. It was my intention to walk the northern section, and while I would prefer to have started not in the middle of the canal, but at its northern end, convenience of transport is my excuse for what I did. The disadvantages were that I had my face turned away from the sun, a shocking waste, and a slightly uphill walk on my first three miles while the canal climbed up 19 locks before reaching the ten mile pound of its summit level from Hudson's Bridge, Lapworth, to King's Norton.

Not only is Kingswood the half-way house between the open and closed sections of the canal; a notice also proclaims it the dividing line between the Trent and Severn Fishery Boards, and as I stood reading that notice a thought struck me. Scorn a canal if you will, but shut your eyes and the trickle of water which usually escapes through closed lock gates might well be a mountain stream. And where are two miles of hill burn with the beauty and interest of this flight of locks, their basins populated by graceful swans and erratic moorfowl, blue-black swallows skimming the surface, and reed buntings — the cock conspicuous with his black head and white collar — playing in the rushes; the blue of the bugle in the grass, the tracery of chervil in the hedgerows; and the call of the cuckoo loud in the land. A narrow boat, obviously in the process of conversion, shrouded with tarpaulins, lay in one short pound. Three girls' bicycles were propped against the hedge beside it, an intriguing sight, and I wondered how the occupants could stay abed on this sublime morning.

The flight of locks was ready for any boat locking up, the bottom gate open, the top closed. The top gate of each lock was single, the bottom a pair, meeting in the middle — their advantage being a shorter sweep when opening or closing, thus leaving more room in the lock. Several 'nick bridges' carried the towpath from side to side of the canal, their two cantilever sides failing to meet by a narrow slit through which a tow rope can be passed.

Past the great solid balance beams of the closed lock gates I tramped uphill to the lock-keeper's cottage which made the perfect picture in the early sunlight as I approached it. Of red brick, it stands beside a little nick bridge with a lock behind it and a row of militarily erect black poplars bordering the canal. The basin fronting the cottage has all the appearance of a natural pool, and was the home of a cabin cruiser of doubtful vintage and off-white hue.

John Edwards was astir. He came to the Stratford Canal from the chalk country of the Kennet & Avon Canal in 1925. His job is to conduct all craft through his locks — last year this had amounted to only eight commercial boats, but pleasure craft are booming. As lock-keeping is obviously not a full-time occupation, Mr Edwards spends his days with the repair boat, on general canal maintenance, hedging, and clearing banks and towpath. Last year four single and two pairs of double lock gates had been replaced by the repair gang; this year, so far, two singles. And I learned that the canal was dredged in 1950.

Not content with spending his working day on the water, Mr Edwards' off-duty concern is with the waters under the earth. He is a water diviner, and produced a map of his immediate locality criss-crossed with red and blue pencil lines which indicate polluted and pure underground streams he has traced with his hazel twig. He has several wells to his credit at nearby farms.

Taking my leave with a promise to return for a demonstration of dowsing one evening, I soon saw ahead one of those red symbols like the ace of diamonds which rise above hump-backed bridges to warn against excessively heavy traffic, and are often the boatman's first warning of a bridge, standing, as they do, angular and alien against the sky, where so often the gracefully curved bridge is overhung, mellowed, and merged by time and nature in the green frothiness of leaves and branches.

Church bells rang across the pastures, each proclaiming the whereabouts of a village. The grey spire of Lapworth church appeared ahead. A mouselike wren, going into hiding on a lock-gate beneath the balance beam, chirruped its heart out — a little brown bird singing. But a more sinister sound rent the morning, the low whine ascending to a banshee wail from an airfield some miles distant of Vampire jets, sucking the peace of the Sabbath into their infernal maws and shattering it.

Beyond Hudson's Bridge — a stone structure, and canal employees will always correct you if you refer to it as brick — the road to Hockley Heath runs alongside the canal, a fact which gave me comfort when a swan, which had inconsiderately built its nest across the towpath, disputed my passage. I turned back and took to the road, happily with no witness to my discretion, rejoining the canal at a drawbridge which gives access to Drawbridge Farm.

The farm belongs to the Lapworth Charities, and thither, 95 years ago, went Thomas Cranmer, though Cranmers first appear in the parish register in the 1560s. Grand-children of Thomas, William and Ellen Cranmer, now inhabiting the farmhouse, told me how the canal brought the bricks to build local houses some 50 years back, and more recently shrubs for Mr Jefferson's gardens at Lapworth House.

The dew was still wet on my path. Fern-like leaves gave promise of drifts of meadowsweet to come, fronds of tansy spoke of yellow buttons which would stud the summer, and curlicues of vetch augured their purple patches. The white flowers had come first – upright garlic mustard known to country children as Jack-by-the-hedge, and stars of stitchwort while silky rush flowers fringed the water. An almighty disturbance, starting among the rushes and leaving a wake of churned-up water half way across the canal was probably a rat, for a moment later I saw another, swimming below the surface parallel with the towpath.

Hockley Heath achieved more importance from the canal in bygone days than it can now claim as it stands astride the main Birmingham – Stratford road. Indeed, its ancient status was shown in the title of the Hockley Port Association for the Prosecution of Felons, that forerunner of the police, formed in January 1797, doubtless for protection against the 'navvies' engaged in cutting the canal. Wharf Lane still recalls the days when non-perishable goods such as stone, brick, timber, lime, coal, and salt came by canal for distribution over considerable tracts of countryside. J.J. Belton, Hockley Heath's historian, tells us that the last load to be brought to the wharf — Enoch's Wharf as it is called — was on Christmas Eve, 1929.

Pleasure may inherit what commerce began in the canals of Britain, and tied up at Wharf Lane bridge was STENTOR, the narrow boat belonging to Mr R.H. Lee, chairman of the Midlands branch of the Inland Waterways Association. Compared with NORMAN CHAMBERLAIN she seemed deficient in windows, but as she probably has fewer people aboard to shut them on approaching a tunnel, where they can be so easily wrenched off, the shortage may have its advantages.

Another drawbridge, and the canal entered a cutting which brought me beneath the main road bridge to the hump where the towpath crosses an arm behind the Wharf Inn which once led into the salt warehouse. This has now disappeared; the arm is partially filled in, but in what was left lay a punt with, of all things, an outboard motor.

From the back gardens of a row of cottages where Tapps or Taffs Wharf once stood on the Umberslade Road, two particularly obnoxious dogs yapped and snarled at me across the canal as it turned north-west. A spot around the next bridge is known as Sadlerswells, and there I executed several movements unknown to ballet as a second, far from dying, swan showed a hissing and disconcerting interest in my trouser leg.

Violets and bluebells now added to the flora. The surrounding landscape opened out again to pleasant prospects after a spell of enclosed towpath, and at Rotherham's Oak Farm the canal also opened out, wide enough, I thought, to 'wind' a boat. The uninitiated may not realise what a problem it is on a canal to turn in one's tracks. A narrow boat is most awkward going astern, so this is impossible over any distance, and with a 70 foot length to turn ('wind' pronounced like that which blows is the correct term) in a canal one third that width is equally impossible. The boatman who takes a wrong turning raises no end of a problem for himself, as winding places are miles apart.

My indignation at the outboard motor on the punt was

inflamed again when, moored at a pretty and colourful cottage with japonica on the walls and tulips bordering the lawn, I saw a boat meant for rowing again cumbered with this lazy device, and named PAL. At Illshaw Heath the populace was cultivating its garden, which activity was punctuated by regular splashes in the canal as stones and grass hurtled over the hedge to the danger of passers-by and the detriment of the waterway. This method of disposal of garden rubbish is very prevalent, and should be discouraged with a tidy fine or two. But Illshaw Heath gave me a boyhood memory as an orange-tipped butterfly settled on a dandelion, that most maligned harbinger of summer and gloriously golden of flowers.

Over 30 years ago my grannie lived — and died — in a canal-side cottage at Illshaw Heath, and one of the novelties of visiting her was that the butterflies, which were white in our town garden, had orange tips to their wings. Almost as a vote of thanks to my long memory from the order *Lepidoptera,* a peacock butterfly joined me and fluttered ahead for half a mile, settling every few minutes to display its beautiful roundels. I promise to remember it should I walk this way again in another 30 years. It was in this stretch of canal that I first saw my father swim.

Under a bridge beneath the Bluebell Inn, past cheerful red farms on verdant pastures, a sight of Earlswood Church, and so to a long straight reach that made my hands itch for a boat's tiller. Stalks of wood spurge were now hanging narcissus-like over the canal; a cackling jay planed from tree to tree; and moorfowl dabbled. At the feeder from Earlswood — the summit level reservoirs — two men were working in their own little boatyard, Joseph Noble on his pontoon conversion STELLA which has already cruised Avon and Severn, and Robin Tipping with his 16-foot cabin cruiser on which he has done 131 miles in a week's single-handed journey over North Midlands canals. He calls his craft QUO VADIS.

Then, blades flashing rhythmically in the sun, came Peter Jackson in a 15-foot rigid two-seater canoe WANDERLUST. He pays dues of £2.6s.8d. per year to the Docks & Inland Waterways Executive, and keeps his canoe in a shed at an old wharf along with those of two of his friends. The closed southern section of the canal has no terrors for Peter who has canoed to Stratford, portaging round the locks. When I came abreast of his old wharf it was to realise again how many weird craft one sees afloat are ancient bus tops, for here they lay, and here lay an old bus or two awaiting a new lease of life on a new element.

A third drawbridge spans the canal, with a nearby stores and pub named after it, and at this point the derelict Priory Windmill, bereft of sails, looms ahead. Extensive sandpits yawn red on the left as a short aqueduct carries the waterway 30 feet above the River Cole and a road. A rowing boat is propelled inexpertly by two youths. Suburbia and the populous parts of the canalside await us. Two inconspicuous barns on the far bank once housed the first aluminium works in the country. A deep cutting where the water is of a bilious syrupy green, takes the canal through Yardley Wood to the huge Birmingham Corporation bus garage now dominating Happy Valley, once a place of crowded Bank Holiday resort. The Berrys are sole survivors of four families which let out rowing boats in those days before a municipal estate encroached on haunts where I regularly saw a kingfisher. Behind the Three Horse Shoes Inn on Alcester Road bridge, an ancient arm disappears into the undergrowth, well adapted to the delivery of barrels in earlier days.

We are within two miles of the junction with the Worcester Canal, but still there remain three interesting features. First, the 352 yards Brandwood End Tunnel, with two niches well adapted to holding statues, but used only for adventurous climbers to paint their initials, at the east portal. Following the horse path beside the grounds of Monyhull Hall Colony, and crossing a main road, I dipped down to the canal where it emerges, to find two identical niches at the west portal, with a representation of a human face in a panel between them. Brindley? Telford? Bridgewater? — one of the great names of canal engineering? No, a far greater. No less, though weathering renders identification difficult, than William Shakespeare. After all, it is the Stratford-on-Avon Canal!

Then a swing bridge. In 1946 the future of the canal depended on this structure. The Great Western Railway, owners of the canal, erected a fixed bridge which prevented all traffic passing on the canal. When it seemed the Stratford Canal was doomed, the Inland Waterways Association brandished its emblem, Excalibur, and claimed right of way. The question went to Parliament; the swing bridge replaced the fixed bridge, and the canal was saved.*

Not only saved but revived. As I write, a party of 300 waterways enthusiasts in five narrow boats in tow of a tug has just spent a Sunday cruising the canals from Gas Street Basin, Birmingham, to Earlswood — first of a series of commercial pleasure cruises on local canals.

Third and last of these features is the guillotine lock already described, the only one of its kind in the country, and as such a heritage which must be preserved. At the junction, before an old toll house, stands a canal signpost, its three arms pointing to Worcester, to Birmingham, and back to Kingswood whence we have come.

Heavy overnight rain instead of dew had watered the towpath eleven days later when I set out from Kingswood again, this time with my face turned southward to walk the 13 miles of the lower or southern section to Stratford-upon-Avon; and John Edwards was standing in a cumbersome rectangular boat in the dank depths of a lock, tearing yellow trefoil, bramble, and other plants from crevices in the damp walls. this time my way lay downhill, and the turf was springy enough to give an impetus to my feet so that as I hurried past the seven Lapworth locks my progress resembled that of the stream on my left rather than that of the canal on the other hand. Only the towpath and a hawthorn hedge separated the two, but while the brook rippled its speedy way to join the River Alne, the canal pursued a placid course, stepping downward with dignity from pounds like charming natural pools through the regular locks with single gates both top and bottom. It mirrored the willows on the far bank, while the near water's edge was fringed with sedges and the lance-shaped leaves of water plantain with last year's flower stalks, black and brittle, protruding well beyond them.

A beautiful clear pound of some length succeeded the Lapworth locks. At the top of Lowsonford's five I ran into a hostile reception

* see footnote on page 73.

from a goose with three goslings outside Walter Freeman's cottage, a nettled ditch beside the towpath leaving little room to take avoiding action. The various canal companies had their peculiar architecture for stores and lock cottages, and on this lower section there are some half dozen long, low, barrel-roofed dwellings now housing canal pensioners. Walter's furniture came to this retreat by canal boat 40 years ago, and there it seems likely to stay until it disintegrates in the absence of water transport to remove it, while Walter beautifies the surroundings of his home with an array of polyanthuses and wallflowers, and continues to live off the land.

He was busily feathering some rooks — spoil of a shoot the previous evening — in a garden where the skin of a badger he had killed swung from a line to scare birds off the pea rows. When I asked if the rooks were intended for a pie, grey-haired comfortable Mrs Freeman invited me into her living room to see a pastry bowl already half full of legs and breasts. The whitewashed barrel roof rendered the room surprisingly lofty, and it led into a bedroom from which yet another opened out along the length of the building, while another door from the first bedroom gave onto a third, constructed from a stable and used as guest room by various of Mrs Freeman's 14 children, all still alive, on their visits.

When Walter Freeman first came to the canal on maintenance work, they would take a load of bricks and cement aboard the repair boat and push off to operate on walls and locks until their supplies were exhausted, and good workmen they must have been, judging from the present state of preservation of the canal brickwork.

Waving farewell to the Freemans, I was soon passing between the stone piers which once carried the bridge with the track of the Lapworth – Rowington Junction – Henley Railway, a venture, begun in 1861 but abandoned through lack of funds within five years, which the Great Western took up later, completed, and opened to passenger traffic in the summer of 1894. Its purpose was somewhat negatived by the opening of the North Warwickshire line between Birmingham, Henley, and Stratford on July 1, 1908. The earlier line was connected with the new one by the bridge crossing the main Birmingham – Stratford road, and trains from Lapworth ran into the new Henley station. A much reduced passenger service continued on the older line after 1908, to be abandoned in January 1915. Goods traffic survived another year, but on January 1, 1917 the track was officially closed and dis-mantled — the metals being intended for the Western Front.

At Lowsonford, a typical Arden village two miles south of Kingswood, the canal washes the lawns behind the Fleur-de-Lys Hotel. There, almost obliterated by a large hawthorn, is a very ancient lamp rising from the bank, which must have shone a welcome beacon to boatmen in the days of the canal's comparative prosperity.

The slow tempo of village life infected me as I strolled through Lowsonford along its dustless watery highway. I leaned con-templatively over a fence to watch a mare with her stringy foal, and from behind a hedge another mare came into view accompanied by twin brown foals. Yellow Jersey cows with sooty faces cropped in the pasture on the offside, while in an adjacent field to the horses on the towing path side complacent Herefords stood contentedly knee-deep in buttercups.

Another fine broad pound stretched to the three Preston Bagot locks. Lowering clouds had come up threateningly from the south, and a shrewd wind ruffled the water into wavelets, and brought country sounds from the fields — an anonymous hammering, the chug of several tractors, and the imbecile laugh of a woodpecker which revealed itself as of the great spotted variety, rarer in Warwickshire than the more attractive green woodpecker. On a grassy field that sloped to the canal a man had placed full sacks in well-spaced symmetry. Regularly the canal was spanned by nick bridges which carried the towpath to the opposite side, possibly to equalise the strain on either side of the horse in towing days, and the short clean turf was always a joy to tread, while nowhere were the hedges rank and uncared for.

The first of three aqueducts on the southern section crosses a brook immediately above Preston Bagot locks — Yarningale

Aqueduct, a cast-iron trough 50 feet long beside another barrel-roofed cottage in the window of which was a trio of kittens, one smoky, one black, and one a tabby.

E. Temple Thurston was enraptured when he passed this way aboard the FLOWER OF GLOSTER, with the Manor House at Preston Bagot, said by some to be the first house built in the Forest of Arden. 'It must be the finest example of half-timbered house there is left in England,' Thurston wrote. 'Leicester's Hospital in Warwick seemed nothing to be compared with it.' I agreed. Red brick is so much more congruous in a lush green countryside than the usual white of half-timbering. There across the canal, framed in trees, and with one tenderly verdant lime before it, it glowed so warmly the wonder was that its timbers did not ignite.

It was at Preston Bagot wharf that True Tilda left Sam Bossom's narrow boat, SUCCESS TO COMMERCE in Q's novel, to move on to her next adventure at Henley-in-Arden with six wooden horses consigned by canal from Birmingham to Preston Bagot for the roundabouts at the Primrose Fête.

A long pound of three miles twisted before me to Bearley Lock, and I now had joint pre-occupations; the weather, which was most menacing, and food. I hurried on, seeking shelter from what threatened, intending to eat my sandwiches in whatever haven I found. The rain began. Ahead across the canal, Kington Farm rose from what was obviously a road dropping from it to the canal. A bend obscured the crossing, but I hoped most fervently that it would be a hump-backed bridge with the towpath running beneath, thus offering the shelter denied me by a stout hedge devoid of trees. My luck was out. It was just another accommodation nick bridge, its piers rising straight from the water and the path switch-backing over it. For a moment I played with the idea of taking off my shoes and socks, rolling up my trousers, and standing in the canal beneath the shelter of the bridge. But the water was too deep.

So, assailed by a minor cloudburst, I scurried to the next nick bridge, which carried a green lane across the canal, and ducked into the undergrowth of alder and hazel beneath an ivy-clad elm into what my little twin daughters call a 'fairy house.' There, in a noble company of 'lords and ladies' clothed in the translucent sheaths of cuckoo pint, with a questing wren and a cock chaffinch as my minstrels, I fed. The rain, which had scarcely penetrated my bower, ceased. At first in dappled shimmering globules, and then in a flood, the returning sunshine illumined the foliage with an aqueous radiance, in Marvell's words —

> "Annihilating all that's made
> To a green thought in a green shade."

Blue skies, with argosies of rolled white cumulus, had succeeded the rain clouds when I strode forth again joyously into the sunshine. Away to my left, mass upon green wavy mass, rose a solid jungle of treetops in Austy Woods, and at my feet on the muddy verge of the canal was a fine specimen — always a rewarding discovery — of celery-leaved crowfoot, one of the smallest of the ranunculus flowers on the bulkiest of stems. Its relative, the marsh-marigold — 'brides of the sun' as the glowing blooms are called by country folk — had been with me all day, brightening the path and cheering my heart. What a colourful world of pleasure is denied those who pass unheeding by the flowers of the wayside and woodland. And how, as I watched a blue-black swallow skim the water, I wished I was as well versed in birds as in flowers.

The white walls and grey roof of the Navigation Inn, Wootton Wawen, half-way house of my day's walk, were now below the embankment where the canal opens out into a winding pool before crossing the Birmingham – Stratford road on an aqueduct 100 feet long. Again, as at Yarningale, the canal is contained in a cast-iron trough for all the world like a wartime static water tank as one crosses beside it on a narrow path with an iron railing high above the road, a fine vantage point to look down into passing cars, often with exciting views of unsuspecting lady drivers' legs.

On Christmas Day, 1940, I had had dinner at the Navigation Inn with my fellow sufferers from searchlight sites dotted around Arden. The aqueduct, running as it does behind the Inn yard, was admirably adapted to the relief of those who imbibed not wisely but too well.

Delightfully clean, and with the aspect of a slow-flowing river so far, the canal deteriorates beyond Wootton Wawen to assume a more stagnant character, with many surface weeds. But at the first nick bridge from the aqueduct, the eye is drawn to one of those entrancing distant horizons many miles westward, which are occasionally framed in a Warwickshire treescape.

Bearley (sometimes called Edstone) Aqueduct, is the great spectacle of the canal. Five hundred feet long, it strides on 14 piers over the Birmingham − Stratford Railway, the disused Bearley − Alcester line, a secondary road, and a tributary of the Alne. Its maximum height is 26 feet. I disturbed its guardian spirit, a mature slate-grey heron, whose ponderous wings as it flew away seemed to span the width of the trough.

The afternoon had become pleasant, with sunny periods and scudding cloud shadows; the water ruffled by a playful wind. Pairs of nesting swans were still to be seen every half mile, and now there were more ducks; mallards, and white domestic birds. Every few hundred yards an accommodation bridge led to a red brick farm — Draper Bridge, Noals Bridge, Featherbed Lane Bridge (named before the Stanley Evans era), Hardwick Bridge, Canada Bridge. But generally the canal continued to traverse lonely country until it ran alongside the railway station at Wilmcote after passing between what appear to have been the abutments of a bridge.

Decay, though far from irreparable, sets in at Wilmcote. The road bridge, in precarious condition, is shored up with stout wooden supports, and some of the pounds between the twelve Wilmcote or Old Stratford locks are dry as they carry the cut down to Bishopton. Mary Arden's House, home of Shakespeare's mother, is only a short step from the dilapidated bridge, but cannot be seen until, turning round some distance through Wilmcote one looks back and across the canal at its black and white timbered front, framed by the limbs of Warwickshire elms. In my opinion the most interesting of the Shakespeare shrines, Mary Arden's House is a fascinating museum of agricultural and domestic implements, many long since forgotten.

Consult any but the best of dictionaries and 'loggat' is missing. Look in the graveyard scene from *Hamlet* and you find 'Did these bones cost no more the breeding, but to play at loggats with them?' Loggats are wooden, truncheon-like objects used in an ancient game of the bowls type, and a set of them with the cheese-like jack, can be seen in the Mary Arden museum. Words are here to challenge the curious: a costrel, a small barrel of cider as part of the farm labourer's hire; an ophicleide, a wind instrument of the tuba type; a goffering iron, for ironing frills and ruffs; lattens, warning bells worn by horses when out after dark; adzes, thatch hooks, eel spears, clap nets for catching sparrows, mantraps, a glover's last. And the dove-cote has 1657 nesting holes.

At Bishopton, less than two miles from the canal's junction with Avon, the one inch O.S. map has its most intriguing entry on the whole length of the canal — 'Royal Victoria Spa, disused.' A tall wall lines the towpath, with the outhouses, lofts and yards of the one-time pump house and hotel on its other side. A fine variety of trees, chestnuts, hornbeams, an ilex, a stately Wellingtonia, and an avenue of lopped limes, embower these buildings raised beside springs of iron and magnesium. Despite the patronage of Victoria as a princess, commemorated in the Royal Arms embossed on the facade, the spa failed, and today the hotel is divided into two separate residences. One, Bruce Lodge, once Bruce Bairnsfather's 'Better 'Ole', has an exciting feature, a large attic with a big window, but with no means of access whatever. In the other lives Mr Reginald Leefe, painter, and theatrical designer, whose mother, though born in New Zealand, was a Warwickshire Arden. The pump room is the charming home of George Goodwin, a Birmingham builder, who collects clocks, whose gardening is rendered hazardous by the regular discovery of wells — eight to date — and who would rather suffer rheumatism than drink the medicinal waters which spring on his property.

The five remaining Stratford locks bring the tally of locks on the southern section to 36, and they contain more water than the Wilmcote flight. On this last lap the canal gives a flow of water to Stratford Gasworks — earlier it had supplied the railway troughs at Rowington, Bearley, and Wilmcote, and throughout its length farms had taken their supplies from it. So the canal is still utilitarian in addition to providing the loveliest walk in the county. And far from pollution in the environs of the town, the water is of crystal clarity where it flows beneath the railway and the Birmingham road; an unfortunate clarity perhaps, because its bottom is the dumping ground for an unsightly collection of metal drums.

So the canal makes a last loop through Stratford to join the Avon in the august surroundings of the Bancroft Gardens before the Memorial Theatre, coming from haunts of rural solitude to a place of crowded resort. Had the intentions of William James reached fruition, Bancroft Gardens would have been a busy inland port instead of a centre of recreation and adulation, and instead of the five Shakespearian characters on the Gower Memorial we might have seen James supported by Thomas Telford, James Brindley, George Stephenson, and Brunel. For not only was William James responsible for the completion of the canal, but in the1820s he projected a 'Central Junction Rail-way or Tram-road' to connect the canal system of the Midlands with the Metropolis. Stratford was to be the railhead, and it is fitting that where rail and water were to join forces in establishing Stratford's commercial prosperity, there stands today a relic of the only portion of James's ambitious rail network to be realised.

This was the Stratford & Moreton Tramway, horse-operated, which was opened in 1826, and one of the ancient trucks still stands on a portion of preserved track at the southern end of Stratford's Tramway Bridge, just across the Avon from the canal junction. Traffic last used the tramway around 1900. The rails were removed in 1918, leaving an interesting 'collector's piece' for those who like to sort out the decaying works of man from nature's obliterating mantle. When the Great Western took over from the Oxford, Worcester & Wolverhampton Railway, it converted part of the old tramway to steam operation as the major length of the Moreton-in-Marsh to Shipston-on-Stour Branch.

As luck would have it, I returned to my desk next morning to a post which included a 'Report of the Stratford-on-Avon Canal Sub-committee' of the Midlands Branch of the Inland Waterways

Association, dated March 1953. It dealt only with the southern section, and was most impressively and lovingly done by a band of rare enthusiasts, the condition of each lock being detailed, the bridges enumerated, the length given of each embankment, and the relevant Acts of Parliament dragged from their obscurity.

On financial considerations concerning the revival of the section, the report said 'Assuming that the waterway was at present in good navigable condition, something of the order of £3,000 per annum would be required to keep it so. As far as direct income is concerned, in the absence of commercial traffic it is doubtful whether anything more than a very few hundred pounds per annum would be realised, and this might well be swallowed up in rents, rates, taxes, and the cost of water.'

A drawback to restoration is, of course, the dead-end nature of the canal, the 16½ miles of the Upper Avon from Stratford to Evesham not being navigable. If some single-minded body could do for the Upper Avon what the Lower Avon Navigation Trust has done for the river from Pershore to Tewkesbury, yet another waterway would be open from Birmingham to the sea.

As it is, the canal looks like remaining an Arcadian paradise for ramblers and botanists. The collection of flowers with which I invariably end a country excursion included, in addition to my celery-leaved crowfoot, some bitter cress — a white flower which vies and may even be confused with the pale pink lady-smock along many miles of the canal banks, yellow rocket, yellow archangel, marsh valerian, and some fine spikes of bugle which is most prolific.

CHAPTER FIVE

In which NORMAN CHAMBERLAIN *finds new canals to conquer, and we travel on the Grand Union to the Coronation of Queen Elizabeth II*

In my wartime Royal Artillery battery we had a chap who was a canal boatman in happier days. At the useful accomplishment of taking a boat and her butty through a lock, and moving some 50 tons of goods from London to Birmingham he was an expert. At the imbecile exercises with feet and rifles which afflicted us during military service he was more than usually clumsy. One manoeuvre he never mastered was that of stepping backward when opening or closing order without a startled glance over his shoulder to see that he, who could propel a 70-foot narrow boat with nicety into a lock, was propelling himself into the proper gap. On parade one day he was in the front rank, and after the battery commander had satisfied himself on the stupid details for which he was inspecting us, the sergeant-major shouted "Close order, march." Bill took his customary look backward and shuffled into position.

"Have that done again, sergeant-major," said the battery commander. Again we opened and then closed ranks. Again Bill looked apprehensively over his shoulder.

"What's the matter with that man?" demanded the irate B.C. The sergeant-major — the best in the British army — thought quickly.

"Well sir," he explained. "Nixon's a boatman, and he's been brought up never to step backward without looking for fear of falling in the canal". The B.C. was not amused.

Nixon had probably been released for the Forces by one of the girls of the Ministry of War Transport Women's Training Scheme for canal boats. In teams of three, nicely-nurtured girls and women trained and worked a pair — motor and butty — on the Grand Union Canal from London to Birmingham, Coventry,

Leicester, and Nottingham. A man-sized job this, with oil, mud, and rats, where their sisters in the Armed Services had the glamour of uniforms. Two, at least, of the women wrote books about their experiences, and good books they were. First, in 1947, came Susan Woolfitt, wife of Sir Donald, with *Idle Women* — excellent in every way and invaluable for its Grand Union lore. A year later Emma Smith published her famous *Maidens' Trip,* rather whimsical and too consciously literary at the expense of down-to-earth canal stuff. Someone must have suggested to her that she would sell better with fiction than fact. So she resorted to the trick of using herself as a character, Emma, always in the third person. This might have been bearable, but always in the plural she writes in the first person of 'we', meaning Emma and her mates, Charity and Nanette.

When Paul decided to take NORMAN CHAMBERLAIN to London for the Coronation in May 1953 with 12 boys and 4 adults, I saw

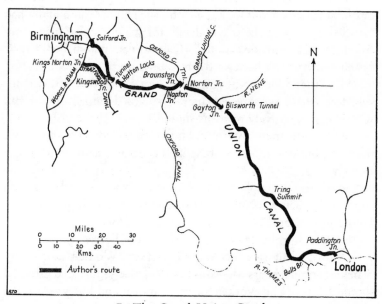

7: The Grand Union Canal

the perfect chance of doing my south-eastern journey, so signed on with the alternatives of sleeping on the floor, beneath hedges, or in whatever canalside accommodation I could find. Since NORMAN CHAMBERLAIN had pioneered the way for canal boats with boys' clubs, four more were afloat or in process of conversion, ERNEST THOMAS at Wolverhampton, and others at Greet's Green, Leicester, and Oxford. Now we were to blaze the trail to London.

It was a forbidding overcast morning on May 28 when we left King's Norton basin at 10 a.m. I felt sorry for the solitary boy who leaned over the first bridge at the junction as we winded to set our nose towards Kingswood. In the basin there had been the Vicar to bless our voyage, the B.B.C. to record our departure, rival journalists to write of it, and boys' club officers to say "Cheerio". Now only 200 yards away was this one lonely lad on a bridge, maybe envying our good fortune. But when we fished up a kettle on our shaft he laughed as loudly as we did, and we set out on the 12 miles of the upper section of the Stratford-on-Avon Canal, described in the last chapter.

There were two unfortunate innovations aboard. One boy had brought a gramophone with the most horrifying collection of jazz records, another a wireless set of equally low musical taste. Adding to the discord, Paul had a Tannoy loud-hailer over which he informed all and sundry of our origins and intentions: "This is NORMAN CHAMBERLAIN, the narrow boat of Birmingham Boys' Clubs, going to London for the Coronation." This brought out wondering and envious-eyed children to back garden fences against the canal, and their mothers to shout their good wishes.

At the first drawbridge one little girl was so attracted to our boat that she cycled slap into the rushes and stood on her head with legs kicking while she slowly sank through into the water. Ken Guest, a young solicitor's clerk, reached the towpath with a prodigious leap from mid canal and tore back to extricate and soothe her.

Walking this towpath a month earlier I had wondered how NORMAN CHAMBERLAIN would fare in waters so little used. Taking the tiller I soon knew. First we had to unravel a forest of branches which had attached themselves to our rudder. Thus freed, the rudder began scraping the bottom, causing the tiller to jerk and kick while churning up a black evil-smelling mud which brought round us a cloud of mosquitoes. With the rudder on the bottom steering is impossible, and on one occasion we hit the bank and demonstrated to some of our innocents the dangers of sitting on the fore-peak. Somehow one avoids falling in the cut and bashing one's head on bridges, but there is the ever-present danger, more insidious, of being driven remorselessly into a thorn bush which becomes apparent too late to take evasive action.

A collision with the bank takes a regular form — an anxious frown from the steerer as he recognises the possibility and tries to avert it; a rapid twirl of the little wheel to cut down speed when it becomes inevitable; a shout from someone "Hold tight on top", and another "Watch out below". Then there is a frantic grabbing of loose crockery if a meal is afoot. At last the impact — a dull thud and a rebound if the nose takes the bump high up; grinding and an upward tilt if the keel climbs on stones; a tearing and wailing if trees sweep the forepeak.

I was steering with the tiller in the lower position for the first time. A butty tiller — and NORMAN CHAMBERLAIN was a butty — is a curved length of gaily-painted wood which fits into a socket at the top of the rudder post. Always in the past we had used it curving upward. This has dangers beneath low bridges and in locks, but its advantage on a boat with raised superstructure on which several bodies are always draped is that the steerer can hold the tiller while standing on the gunwales high enough to peer over the obstructions. The lower position, usually adopted on working butties, is undoubtedly better, but it necessitates standing low in the well — an impossibility on NORMAN CHAMBERLAIN if you would see where you were going. I solved the problem by standing upright on the gunwales and clutching the tiller between my knees. This worked well on a straight stretch, but to negotiate a sharp bend I had to dismount and use my hands, getting a glimpse ahead when I could.

At Enoch's Wharf, Hockley Heath, we ran through 200 yards of brilliant green pondweed which rapidly closed again in our wake. A long plank lay across the entire width of the canal to contain the weed, and a linesman pulled it aside to let us through to the third drawbridge. These open by windlass, and it is a breathless moment with this Damoclean threat above one's head. So we came to our first lock at Hudson's Bridge — 153 more lay in the 140 miles before us.

John Edwards was waiting with his bike to lock us down, but the boys soon got the idea, and the lock-keeper admitted to his easiest passage down the Lapworth 19. I wandered the towpath with him while he talked of locking lore; of how he keeps the paddles of Hudson's Top Lock raised to maintain a flow of water for the various undertakings down the canal — Stratford Gasworks, the brewery, and the railway; and how he always leaves one gate open at each lock so that anyone or anything falling in can swim out. He also pointed to the row of black poplars beside his cottage, and told me how the third is always a fortnight earlier in bud and leaf than the rest because his well-stream runs beneath it.

Near the bottom of the Lapworth Locks lay the narrow boat ALLEYNE, being converted to a houseboat by Major and Mrs Andrews. The occupants were not at home, but a board on her side read 'Good luck on trip NORMAN CHAMBERLAIN from ALLEYNE'. We were certainly doing well — Stratford Canal passed and 19 locks overcome in two hours. We had no need to envy the locomotive *King Henry VIII* which thundered across our way with the Inter-City train, Birmingham to Paddington in 2½ hours. There is a lock from the higher level of the Stratford Canal to the Grand Union on the short junction arm. This arm could have been made on the level, but the Warwick & Birmingham (forerunner of the Grand Union) as the earlier canal, insisted on taking a lock of water from the newer cut for each boat to pass the junction.

At 5.30 p.m. we cruised into the Grand Union and, with more water to play in, promptly went on the mud where we lay with a lively breeze showering us with a confetti of may-flower petals. After some shafting and rope-throwing we were bow-hauled off and tied up for tea. The Grand Union consists of over 300 miles of waterways, comprising the main line from Birmingham to London, with branch connections to Slough, Aylesbury,

Northampton (which connects with the River Nene and so through Wisbech to The Wash), and Market Harborough (this last from the Leicester Section which, running to Nottingham, links with the Trent and thus connects Thames and Humber). The amalgamation which formed the Grand Union took place in 1929 and involved the Grand Junction (opened 1793), Warwick & Napton (1794), Grand Union (1810), Regent's (1812), Hertford Union (1824), Birmingham & Warwick Junction (1840), and, two years later, the Loughborough & Leicester Navigation and the Erewash Canal.

The Regent's Canal Dock on the north side of the Thames at Limehouse can accommodate boats of 3,000 tons gross. Their cargoes can be discharged direct into narrow boats for the Midlands, and most of the boats travelling to Birmingham carry timber or metal ingots which are unloaded at Tyseley or Sampson Road wharfs, where still can be seen a flourishing canal life.

It was into a green and golden Warwickshire evening that we cruised after tea, on waters shimmering in the sunlight — an elm-studded countryside with meadows of buttercups from which the cows had gone to the milking in cosy red barns. One timbered house on our right, somewhat below the canal, was a gem, its upper windows giving glimpses of beamed rooms. Hereabouts Ken and Vic pole-vaulted ashore on the long shafts to push us off the mud on the cut side (the side without a towpath). The snag in shoving from the bank is that usually the shovers are left ashore, as in this case. Heaving the poles back to us they scrambled through hedges and climbed fields in search of a convenient place to come aboard, preferably a bridge with bricked side and a clear channel. Nothing was forthcoming, and with a deepening wooded cutting and Shrewley Tunnel ahead we had to risk sticking again to close in and take them off.

Shrewley Tunnel, only 433 yards, has an unusual feature in the horse tunnel high up the hill. We came out into the evening glow again, and within two miles were at Hatton Top Lock. There are 21 Hatton Locks and their balance beams stretched across the descending towpath like rods in a giant's staircase, their white ratchet sleeves upright and shining bright. To our right the railway looped round to Warwick, dominated by St. Mary's graceful tower away down the valley, while nearer and to leftward rose the chimneys and turrets of Hatton Mental Hospital.

Before beginning the descent we listened to a broadcast recorded at our departure ten hours earlier, and twitted Paul for his contribution to it. Then we bent many willing backs to a task which is said to take a loaded boat two hours. With their experience in Lapworth Locks the boys quickly mastered the routine of locking down a 'bad road' — the boatman's term for adverse locks. Run ahead to close the bottom gate, open paddles of top gate with windlass, the lock fills so close paddles, open top gate and nose boat in, raise paddles of bottom gate until water inside lock is low as next pound, strain on balance beam and open bottom gate, boat chugs out, drop bottom paddles and leave bottom gate open — a 'good road' for boats locking up. No mystery if you use a little reason. These locks are double to take motor and butty side by side, or 'breasted up'. The particular danger to avoid when locking down is that of resting the stern of the boat on the stone sill of the top gate, thus leaving it high and dry. Unsupported by water the boat could break its back.

The sun had sunk into a cloud bank that boded ill for the morrow, but still its colours on the few clouds overhead were reflected as a dull copper in the still pounds. We closed the last lock gate behind us at 10 p.m., and leaving the Warwick arm on our right, glided beneath the Birmingham Road bridge. A savoury odour of frying sausages and an unsavoury racket from the gramophone rose through the hatches. Paul at the tiller was just a black silhouette with an occasional bat flickering round his head. Such was nightfall on the canal.

We moored alongside the old gaol meadow at Warwick between elms grown 'sombre and human in the twilight', and, across the canal, the conical cypresses of a graveyard whence came, siren-like, the voice of an unseen female to lure us on to a better mooring at 'The Cape of Good Hope', a famous waterside pub. Unheeding, we drove home our mooring stakes and tied up. A full moon sat mistily, like Humpty-Dumpty, on a long low cloud. This was peace. The sausages called, and we were just going below to enjoy them when, from the main road bridge came a loud screech, a whirligig and tumble of headlight, and the shape of a car skidding and spinning madly. We ran to it. With a mercy undeserved by the driver, who reeked of beer, the car had remained on even keel and hit nothing but the grass verge. In the last 20 minutes he had moved as far as NORMAN CHAMBERLAIN had moved in 12 hours and had seen nothing — mere movement, not travel. But for miraculous luck the driver would have seen nothing ever again, which would not have mattered twopence, but that he might have killed or injured some innocent passer-by.

Friday morning set the pattern for our rising throughout the voyage. From whatever slumbers I had contrived on the galley floor I was awakened by Len Lane, the cook, around 5.45 a.m. and hastened to fold my blankets and vacate his domain. Such a premature reveille had its advantage. While Len made a brew of tea, I was in undisputed possession of the wash basin, for which competition became fierce half-an-hour later, and my ablutions were just about done in time for our other early riser, Alan Baker, to take over. Paul would then emerge from the forward cabin to pick a sleepy-eyed way over blankets which had fallen during the night from the still slumbering figures on the wire mattresses either side of the saloon. In the engine-room astern he would perform some rite with grease points, and then rev up. Someone would tumble out to work the first lock — we usually moored near one — and by the second or third there was a complete locking watch of four on duty. The 12 boys were divided into three watches, Red, White, and Blue, each doing 24 hours duty on fatigues. Irrespective of duty each watch was responsible for 10 locks at a time.

This Friday morning we swabbed decks before leaving our mooring, an activity which attracted a gallery of black and white Friesians to watch our departure. Soon we were at the two Warwick Locks by 'The Cape of Good Hope', where we filled up with water, not beer. The pub faces in to the canal, and seats and tables outside enable customers to watch the waterborne traffic as they drink. The little cul-de-sac which ends at the canal was gaily dressed in Coronation bunting. While we filled our tank from the tap in a little brick sentry-box I was interested in the narrow boat conversion CHRISTINE across the canal.

Casting off we managed to hit the lower gate of the second lock hard enough to tip John Austin's cup of tea into his lap as he breakfasted below. Then followed a five-mile pound, under the Kenilworth Road, behind the gelatine factory, successor to George Nelson of Rock Mill, Emscote, who invented gelatine in 1837, and beneath the low bridge at Emscote on a most awkward S-bend. An aqueduct took us over the Avon, and the tower of All Saints, Leamington Spa, loomed through the trees ahead, more squat than St. Mary's which now displayed its slender beauty to best advantage back above the roofs of Warwick. Another aqueduct, and we were over the railway with electricity pylons striding across the fields on our right — a field of charlock, paler yellow than the buttercups. Then came Leamington Rugby Football Club ground, its tall tapering posts rising above a herd of cattle placidly cropping the lush late Spring plenty where stirring battles are fought in a sea of mud on pouring winter afternoons.

A mop is thrust from a hatch and twirls a Catherine wheel of greasy water; a boy leans out to empty bottles of milk which had gone sour into the cut. Our steady progress sucks water from the banks uncovering the flotsam and jetsam of the canal — an old bicycle, a wicker basket, oil drums, a battered toy motor-car, a woman's brassière, dead fish, a limp glossy magazine, deflated contraceptives — dragging them all into the turbulent waves in our wake.

A pungent gasworks' smell greeted us in Leamington, and Paul had his best audience yet at Clemens Street Bridge: "This is the NORMAN CHAMBERLAIN, etc". We pulled alongside for a while and the boys did 15 minutes shopping in the town. Then, the dilatory photographer we were expecting not having arrived, we scrawled a chalk message for him on the bridge buttress, and chugged on. In addition to the usual coarse mural artistry and comment on all blank spaces, canal bridges are a means of communication between boats, and canal friends know of one another's movements by such chalked information as 'TAURUS gone to Tyseley, 11 a.m. Saturday.' As we set off from Clemens Street we met our first working boats,

GAINSBOROUGH and SAVERTON. So we dodged round the far from royal and spa-like back streets of Leamington and were soon in the country again. I took a long spell at the tiller as we climbed up Radford Locks, our first 'up' locks, and we shot up as though jet-propelled when the paddles were opened. The boat seemed sluggish in answering the helm until I changed to the lower position when all went well.

The transition from town to the rolling south Warwickshire hedgerow country was immediate. One of the boys who had been locking brought some may-flower aboard and precipitated a story from Paul about the superstition, which he attributed particularly to Somerset, that this sweet-smelling blossom is unlucky. Seemingly may-flower was picked for decoration by the old Roman Catholics to honour the Virgin Mary. With the Reformation and the persecution of Catholics it was assumed that anyone with may in the house was a fair subject for persecution therefore it was unlucky.

A bridge took the Roman Fosse Way over us near Bunker's Hill Farm with its reminder of history on the far side of the Atlantic. At Welsh Road, named after the ancient cattle-droving route from Wales to London, two gaily-painted narrow boats were locking down, NANCY and NELSON of the Inland Waterway Cruising Company. An assembly of comfortable-looking ladies was seated in the forward well-deck of NANCY enjoying a holiday for which they had paid 10 guineas a week in double, or 11 guineas in single cabins. These boats cruise along a three-pointed star centred on Long Buckby, to Warwick, Market Harborough, and Leighton Buzzard. All passenger sleeping accommodation is aboard the butty NELSON, four double and four single cabins. The dining cabin is forward on the motor NANCY, and the whole set-up is indicative of the growing interest in canals as a source of pleasure.

After an exchange of greetings, newspapers, and brochures we continued up, they down. Radford top lock at Bascote is a double lock, not in the sense that two boats can lie in it side by side, but in that it is two separate locks, the top gate of the lower being the bottom gate of the higher. So much water is used by the two locks that to prevent an excessive drain on the long pound above there is a side pond at the locks. From such a pond water can be taken when locking up, and into it can be emptied water from the lock when locking down. Thus a considerable amount of water shuttles to and fro from locks to side pond without draining away to the lower pound. Before the Grand Union amalgamation most of the locks on its constituent parts were narrow. These now lie derelict beside the broad ones which are of recent date, 1934, and impressive masonry.

From the two-mile pound between Bascote and Stockton locks the white smoke from the chimney of the cement and lime works at Southam is prominent above and among the trees to the right. One boy was amusing himself by throwing lighted fireworks into the canal and watching their torpedo-like behaviour. His first was a thunderflash. He was seated on the forepeak and, lighting it, dropped it overside without any malice aforethought. The 70 foot length of NORMAN CHAMBERLAIN brought the unsuspecting Paul at the tiller almost above the firework when it exploded. Hurriedly he revved down and stopped the boat, prepared, it seemed, to order "Abandon ship". Explanations made, we gathered speed again, the skipper mightily relieved.

My greatest interest was in the enamelled flash of our first kingfisher and of finer weather overtaking us from northward. This was bringing a very cold wind, but Alan Baker was trotting along the towpath clad only in white shorts. At Long Itchington we passed between the white-fronted Two Boats Inn on the left and the yellow-faced Cuttle Inn just off the towpath. Another interesting pub name confronted us in a mile, the 'Blue Lias'. Beyond it at the foot of Stockton Locks three men were swinging scythes rhythmically at a forest of chervil beside an old lime kiln — hence the 'Blue Lias'. We passed KESTREL and CRUX on Stockton, and the brown-faced woman, opening the locks for her husband at KESTREL's tiller, told me that they were bound for Cartwright's Wharf, Acocks Green, with a cargo of timber. This delighted me, Cartwright's being the wharf mentioned in my introduction, across the fields from the canal where I take my children to play.

At the top of Stockton Locks work was in progress on lock gates. In addition to normal 70-foot maintenance boats there was a 'flat', a long strong punt-like craft with a tall cabin used for working in locks. Above the locks was the too-familiar sight of an old butty, waterlogged and with a luxuriant crop of rushes growing from its interior. I have seen trees, alder and ash, rooted in the timbers of such old has-beens. At a bridge near the top lock was another Boat Inn. These pubs were the canal equivalent of the coaching houses on the roads.

I have vivid memories of the first railway journey I did during wartime with my 15-month-old son. His running commentary on the passing scene was 'Buttercups', 'Amoos, no Buttercups', 'Buttercups and Amoos' or any other variation of the two words as each field had its quota of cows and buttercups or neither. For it was late Spring. The same commentary could well be applied to a canal journey through rural Warwickshire with both cows and buttercups more in evidence than not, and with a feeling of less detachment from them than on a train. But among the cattle that raised inquisitive heads as we glided beside their pasture the most remarkable were those at Hill Farm, Leamington Hastings. Like Highland cattle they were as to their long horns, but without the shaggy coats, and lankier with brown bodies and white legs. I learned from a lock-keeper that they are the almost extinct breed of Warwickshire Longhorns.

After lunch we were in country of wider views from Napton windmill to Daventry wireless masts. I sat on my favourite perch, right at the forepeak — a delightful isolated position; my companions forgotten, just the red nose of the boat and the rope fender below my knees; first man round bends, through bridge holes, into locks, and first through the opening gates into new pounds. The friendly chug of the engine reaches me — put-put-put — from 70 feet away on the wind which follows astern, raising little waves to run along the canal with us. There is a kind of bronco-ride in each lock as first the nose hits and mounts the sill, then as the paddles are raised and the water boils and churns up, buffeting the boat in a space meant for two until we are as high as the upper pound. Then our engine coughs into life again, the fender noses the gates open, and we emerge.

At a bend beside two reservoirs we got the wind abeam and were pushed into the lee bank until we put the wind astern again with a left turn at Napton Junction into the Oxford Canal, over which the Grand Union runs for five miles to Braunston where the Oxford Canal turns northward for Rugby. Our new waterway was of a dirty milky colour on which fish seemed to thrive, for our suction left shoals of silvery minnows high and dry on ledges to be washed to safety again by the following waves. We wound along the contour — the Oxford is a Brindley canal, though it was not completed for some years after that great engineer's death — with hedges on the towpath side and sweet pastures running down on the out-side from the little knolls of the Warwickshire – Northants border. But the afternoon was made hideous by ear-splitting records played in lengthy succession by a group of boys, one of whom asked for some playing cards the further to relieve his boredom. All the fields were well furrowed, one having the most comprehensive collection of animals, cows, sheep, horses, even a grey donkey which brayed hilariously to see us — a cacophony preferable to that gramophone.

At one point Terry and Vic went ashore to find a stick for a flagpole. For a mile or more they walked beside the canal seeking an opportunity to board us again, but there was none. Ultimately Paul put the boat in to pick them up, only to run aground in the grey mud which characterises this countryside. We were just too far out to be boarded with comfort, but with the aid of a shaft and risking a ducking they made it successfully. We were still left with the need to get afloat again which no amount of shoving could accomplish. So John Austin and Ken Guest vaulted ashore on the shaft poles and shoved against the boat. This got us going again, but still we had two ashore — albeit a different pair.

As the sun came out later in the afternoon it brought through the hawthorn hedge on our left the delicious smell of an enormous beanfield, and with this still in our nostrils we passed beneath a bridge in a cutting completely obliterated with ivy. Running out of the cutting through fields dusted with the gold of buttercups, we had before us across the London – Birmingham road the spire

of Braunston Church with the red brick tower of a decapitated
windmill beside it, brought to life by a Union Jack straining in the
breeze above it. Just before the road the canal divides, the northern
arm going to Coventry and the notorious 'bottom road'. We
took the arm which continued eastward under the bridge into
Braunston, one of England's most important canal villages.

Braunston boat dock is a microcosm of the colourful canal
world. Here the Nurser family have attained wide fame,
extending even across the Atlantic, as artists in decorated dippers
and cans, the inseparable companions of the black brass-ringed
smoke-stacks on cabin roofs of narrow boats. At the dock the fleet
of Samuel Barlow Coal Company is seen in all its glory of roses,
Carpathian castles, and white rams' heads, those ornate ropes
twisted tightly round the rudder post. Twenty-three pairs
comprise the fleet which carries coal south from the collieries of
the Warwickshire coalfield. Mr le Cheminant, a Guernsey man,
showed me round the dock of which he is manager, the two dry
docks, the tarpaulin shed with its pungent tarry smell, and that
holy of holies where the cans are painted. He spoke of his attempts
to popularise canal cruising; of the butty he let out last summer for
a nominal £3 a week to Sheffield Scouts who camped in her
capacious innards, and of the butty STIRLING which he had recently
converted into STIRLING CASTLE for holidays of a week or fortnight
on Midlands canals similar to those organised by the Inland
Waterways Cruising Company. I learned, too, that to buy a butty
for conversion would cost around £300, when it would be good
enough to last for three years without any overhaul.

Braunston was half way from Warwick, some 20 miles, to our
intended mooring at Stoke Bruerne, so casting off again at 4.30
p.m. we knew we must push along relentlessly through
Northamptonshire, and hoped for a fine evening as, at last, the sun
was winning a battle with the cloud. We were immediately
involved with locks again, less elaborate than earlier ones. The
lower gate at the first bore the date 1877; the upper ones were
dated 1884. Paddle ratchets were no longer enclosed in white
sleeves, but bared their teeth to menace unwary fingers. We filled
our 100-gallon drinking water tank at the first lock and got going

during tea. A bounding breeze came out of the north-west, cleared the sky, and set the branches waving their silvery undersides. Little cottages were fairly frequent at the canal side, stark and not in themselves picturesque, but their red contrasting well with the grey bridges, and in the sparkle of sunlit water all combined to make a joyous buoyant evening.

I enjoy canal tunnels, but pity it was to exchange this fresh air and sunshine for the bowels of the earth. We entered Braunston Tunnel with the good wishes of an old lockman who told us to have a happy time at the Coronation as it might not happen again in our lifetime and certainly not in his. We entered at 6.07 p.m. and could see the far end immediately. It is a dry tunnel with little water percolating through the roof, bigger than those on the Worcester Canal, but the brickwork is not so flush. As we watched the far end growing bigger, a black shape swam into it, a shape with a headlight which outdazzled the brilliant exterior. With John Austin carefully hugging the right-hand wall, we passed a boat close-hauling its butty. A ventilation shaft gave a glimpse of the butty's name — DENTON. The tunnel is 1,868 yards long and our passage took only 17 minutes. We emerged in a cutting with tall beeches rearing their arms far above, and a display of red campion and cranesbill bordering the towpath, but I missed a kingfisher seen by the others. As we chugged into open country, nature assumed a patriotic garb, to the red being added for several miles the blue of scorpion grass, bugle, and speedwell, with the white of chervil and dead nettle.

The Leicester arm of the Grand Union ran to our left at Long Buckby, a placid waterway to be explored one day, far off the beaten track, 20 miles or more with scarcely a village. Just beyond the arm we began descending locks again, and as I trotted along the towing path my long shadow swung to left of us as NORMAN CHAMBERLAIN turned south. All afternoon as we travelled east the Daventry wireless masts had risen on our right. Now they remained there after a 90 degrees turn and were our companions throughout the evening, evidence of the labyrinthine course of the canal.

At 'The Spotted Cow', at Whilton bottom lock, four pairs of

boats were tied up, a cheerful Armada bedecked with Coronation streamers from cratch to cabin, their cargoes small coal. BARROW and TITANIA, TAMWORTH and UNION JACK — inconsequent coupling of names, but coming up were a better related pair, LEOPARD and TAURUS, gunwales deep. Past all this peace, on the rail embankment above a crack train *The Comet* roared Londonwards.

A lovely sylvan stretch ensued, tall black poplars and massive oaks thrusting their topmost boughs to catch the dying rays of evening, while shorter ash, alder, and sycamore overhung the gnat-haunted fish-ringed water. Dense woods and the green twilight of an Amazonian jungle gave place to parkland with a stately home, Brockhall Hall, seen through the gathering dusk. Farming country came in its turn, a wide-winged owl quartering the sleeping pastures.

At Weedon we looped west of Watling Street again for a couple of miles from which an arm, overgrown with rushes and unusable, branches to the right beside the railway station and goes to the Ordnance Depot. We were cruising along an embankment on eye level with the St. George's cross seen dimly on the square tower of Weedon's church. Just beyond, lost in the gathering gloom, were marks on the railway embankment of a rail crash which cost a number of lives rather more than a year ago. The last orange streak of sunset faded. Our searchlight swept the bank ahead disturbing the waterside denizens, mainly moorfowl perching on low overhanging branches. Bob Flint, second lieutenant on the cruise, and I lolled in the open side hatch humming symphonic movements and singing songs. That abominable gramophone was quiet for a while.

At Gayton Junction the Northampton arm melted into the night on our left, and our eyes were skinned for the long Blisworth Tunnel (3,056 yards). Entering it, conditions became much better for Paul at the tiller than in the more confused darkness outside. The passage was uneventful and took only 23 minutes. Driven through an ironstone ridge, the tunnel was a difficult proposition, and during its construction cargoes were transhipped by plate tramway over Blisworth Hill. The leggers who took boats through before the days of engines earned one shilling and six pence per trip, and well they deserved it in their hazardous position on the wings* with only tallow dips, bought at Candle Bridge, to relieve the dripping loom. At least they were spared the diesel fumes which now hang about the tunnel as boats pass under their own power. During the interim between leggers and diesel, a tug towed strings of boats through, and on one tragic occasion its crew of two were found to be dead of suffocation when it emerged after a passage without boats in tow.

It was exactly midnight when we left the murk of the underworld for the more spacious murk outside, and ten minutes later NORMAN CHAMBERLAIN was at her moorings at Stoke Bruerne. In consideration for the crews of working boats already sleeping down by the warehouse facing the Boat Inn, we covered our sledge-hammer with sacking to muffle the noise as we drove home the mooring stakes. Then, with an excellent day of 41 miles and 38 locks behind us, we turned in and slept.

Wind set the keynote of the day on Saturday morning. Buffeting the compact little church tower and tearing at the thatch of Stoke Bruerne village in vain, it hurtled down on the canal to torture the solitary Lombard poplar beside the tall warehouse, and to set the loyal bunting dancing above green and white painted flower boxes on trim lawns close-cropped above the lock. Last night's boats had all departed while yet we slept, and the ruffling waves splashed at the vacant moorings. Serene among the windy tumult the lovely face of our young Queen graced every window. We moved slowly towards the second lock, slightly crab-wise in the gusts, leaving the village behind. The silver windings of the canal beckoned us on into the open country of our coming day's vagabondage, under a cloud-streaked sky which held promise or threat as one was sanguine or apprehensive. The bounding breeze was loud with lark-song and cuckoo-call. It passed across the short pasture leaving it verdant and undisturbed, to sweep up a huge cornfield in wave after misty wave like a drift of the initial powdered snow in the van of a blizzard. Fledgling house-martins

---

*'Wings' were boards temporarily fitted either side of the bows for the leggers to lie on while 'walking' boats through the tunnels with their feet against the tunnel walls.

laboured puzzled into the wind; powerful swifts surged downward on rigid wings breasting the lively water; that aerial acrobat, the lapwing, tumbled more joyously than ever, lifted and blown over the hedges; the kestrel lived up to its other name, the windhover, and remained unmoved; the cuckoo's flight was more than usually erratic; and even the heron's powerful wing beats seemed more ponderous. Five spirited horses galloped across a field to the canal side out of mingled curiosity and joy, their manes and tails streaming downwind.

Seated at breakfast I gazed from the saloon window at the near horizon of a steep meadow where tall grasses did obeisance to the wind, and rabbits sat with cocked ears before dashing over the edge of my world against racing clouds. At bends which put the gale beam on we were forced willy-nilly into the bank, and developed a roll which set utensils sliding down the table-tops to make a case for protective fiddles even in the tranquillity of canal cruising. After one such roll and the grinding of our timbers on the towpath side, I peered out of a hatch to see two boys running hard back towards Stoke Bruerne. They crossed an accommodation bridge and came back to us in the fields on the outside where they were thrown a rope — no mean feat against such a wind — with which they held us in midstream, a frequent expedient in such circumstances. A normal narrow boat, low in the water, is less the sport of the elements than one such as NORMAN CHAMBERLAIN with its long wall of superstructure. So we continued, with engine running but Terry Booth and Peter Hodgson bow-hauling. Complications arose when Terry's cap was blown off and to retrieve it meant abandoning the boat momentarily to the wind. Peter managed to double back, pick up the cap, and return his weight to the rope in time to avert catastrophe.

At a bridge below a wooded hill where a grey church tower was embowered in noisy trees, our bow-haulers came aboard again. Fortunately the church knoll shielded us from the wind for a while as bow-hauling was impossible beyond the bridge where pollarded willows leaned over, their roots half in the canal, half retaining a grip of land, thus barring the passage of a rope. But even having achieved temporary shelter and a fine straight stretch, we still had our troubles when Ken Guest's red tam-o'-shanter was whisked into the canal by a vagrant gust, missed by John's frantic lunge with the boathook, and necessitated putting the owner ashore to go back for it.

In another smother of wind we were able to avoid two pairs of boats bound northward, both empty, high out of the water, and vulnerable. So our day began with the odd incidents of canal travel — three Muscovy ducks waddled ahead and scrambled into a field; a close-shorn round-horned ram looked up lazily and resumed his cropping; showers sprinkled the distant landscape; and now, our constant lodestar as Daventry masts had been the previous afternoon, Hanslope's slender spire rose here, there, and everywhere with its two supporting buttresses.

It was only 9 a.m. but seemed later when we negotiated the one Cosgrove Lock and were faced with an 11½ miles pound to Fenny Stratford — 'Finny' to the boatmen. The old Buckingham arm, unused and blocked by reeds, went off to our right — we were now in Buckinghamshire and heavy rain had overtaken us. With the gale thundering among the chestnut candles above, even the old boatman, crouched beneath his cloth cap at the tiller of BRIAR, observed that it was 'a rough 'un'. Below the lock at Cosgrove, Barlow's NEPTUNE and MARY were waiting beside a dredger. Barlow's boats are easily recognisable apart from being well labelled with the name, by a scroll of roses in white on the bend of the forepeak, and by their colourful 'stands', three masts rising at intervals.

Wolverton Aqueduct, which took us over the River Ouse, once burst and its constructor was charged with manslaughter. The river far beneath, a reedy uncertain stream, drifts away to Stony Stratford, and the canal was within a couple of inches of the top of the aqueduct. At Wolverton, the first town in England to be built entirely as a railway town, was the London & North Western's great workshop for the manufacture and repair of coaches. The canal meanders sharply to the east through New Bradwell, a township devoid of interest but for the ancient tower windmill, its sails gone, but with a wooden cap in fine condition. From the next canal pub, 'The Black Horse', the Bucks Otter Hounds are hunted — curse them!

One of the loveliest views of the journey was St. Andrew's Church at Great Linford, yellow-grey stone with a schoolhouse hard by, its roof shaped like a halberdier's helmet. The canal was well above fields on the left where there were extensive sandpits, and a few hundred yards beyond the church was the Old Wharf Inn, its tables and chairs standing on the towpath. We tied up to water, and the landlord came expectantly to his door just as Len appeared above the hatch with a tray of cups of tea. One hundred years ago there was an arm to Newport Pagnell, whose sturdy tower was visible a mile or so away. Cooper's agricultural implement warehouse is built over the old canal at the junction.

Rain had ceased and a bright sun was sending shadows of contorted clouds scurrying across the meadows, just such a day as might have moved Margaret L. Woods to her verse:

> Sweetest Earth, I love and love thee,
> Seas about thee, skies above thee,
> > Sun and storms,
> > Hues and forms
> Of the clouds with floating shadows
> On thy mountains and thy meadows.

One of the greatest advantages of carrying a home snail-fashion is that you can enjoy nature in its most ominous, brooding, and boisterous moods far in the wilds with complete freedom from weather worries. You can dwell with the gathering storm to the moment it breaks, and greet the first ray of returning sunshine as the branches drop their jewels. For all its nearness to the weather the canal boat is not only the snuggest but the most impregnable of dwellings.

The canal was now winding bewilderingly round the contour and the chimney stacks of a brickworks near Bletchley were appearing in an amazing variety of directions. Near Fenny Stratford the canal was rust red but very shallow, and I stirred up grotesque shapes of black mud steering on the bottom, though in the obvious channel. The banks were lined with many thousands of dead fish, roach, perch, and gudgeon, a shocking sight. Away to the right stretched the pools of old sand and gravel pits where all the youth and beauty of Buckinghamshire disported itself as on a lido during wartime. John took us round the 90 degrees left-hand bend under a bridge beside 'The White Hart' without a touch — a masterly piece of steering — and I caught a glimpse of the gables of Rhondda House, one of my wartime billets. The first lock at Fenny Stratford gave a rise of only one foot, and was said to be necessitated by a surveyor's error in his levels, a mistake he expiated by committing suicide, drowning in the canal.*

I wrote of Fenny Stratford in my wartime diary on June 23rd, 1944: 'It stretches for a short distance along the main Watling Street, equidistant, 44 ½ miles as a signpost outside camp shows, between Coventry and London. West of the road the village, notable for nothing but seven pubs in a row, merges with the pleasant little town of Bletchley. Here is a 12th Century Norman church, where one of the vicar's ancestors was father-in-law to Hogarth, the painter.' Fenny Stratford offsets its obviously abnormal consumption of liquor by producing brewing sugar at the mills of Valentin, Ord, Nagle & Co. which overshadows one of the pubs at the bridge beneath which the Grand Union took us westward of Watling Street again.

A benevolent male citizen of Bletchley leaned over a bridge and remarked "Very nice, have a good time," and as we cruised past a new estate a little girl threw a flower from another bridge. The bloom intrigued me until I found it to be half-a-dozen daisies stuck down the hollow stalk of some other plant. From time to time pairs of boats approached, purposeful black triangles low in the

---

*In fact, the truth, as told by Alan Faulkner in his *The Grand Junction Canal*, is more prosaic. Between Fenny and Wolverton, the canal leaked extensively, the worst length being the 2 miles north of Fenny where it proved impossible to maintain a sufficient depth of water for loaded boats. As a temporary measure, a lock was built at Fenny in 1802 and the pound to Wolverton lowered by about one foot. Since then no-one has risked the expense and disruption which its removal would occasion.

water at a distance, becoming more colourful on closer acquaintance.

On one hairpin bend near Leighton Buzzard we were blown and pinned on a lee shore, and only after most of us were on the towing path with a shaft fore and aft, first pushing and then holding her off, walking along as we did so, could we get going again. I was glad to walk for a mile along the pleasant towpath until a lock gave an opportunity to get aboard again near Leighton Buzzard, which showed up with a bulbous little spire, several side-bits clinging precariously to it; a more normal steeple; and a white skyscraper surmounted by a Union Jack. I took over for a while and was lucky in the shelter of trees as I brought her to a mooring beside some boats at a Little Venice where two or three houses rose direct from the cut. At the bridge we popped up for a brief glimpse of civilisation from which one is isolated on the canal. We left Leighton Buzzard at 5.30 p.m. into an evening still windy, but with sufficient sun to lounge on deck in comfort. All afternoon a wooded hill ridge had been our neighbour to the left. Now we were outflanking it, and the northern ridge of the Chilterns lifted its bare shoulders above gaps in the trees. Poppies, now appearing regularly along the banks, were also a sign of our approach to the chalk, though immediately out of Leighton Buzzard there were capacious brown sandpits bordering our waterway.

The first of the locks to be climbed over the hills filled with startling rapidity, and within two minutes we were nosing forward, leaving beside it the British Waterways ice-breaker THEOPHILIS, a powerful steel boat heavily weighted at the bows. The next lock had a tricky bridge approach with steps just inside the bridge — a risky jump but with a graveyard and chapel conveniently adjacent.

We were now festooned loyally with Union Jacks. A Jolly Roger which fluttered at our forepeak yesterday had not made a reappearance. Every boat had its flags; every little canal girl her hair tied with red, white, and blue ribbon. Soon the Whipsnade Lion was in view, a faithful representation cut in the chalk to the left of Ivinghoe's bold and entrancing crown, and leftward still, over Dunstable Down, a dozen gliders, graceful as gulls, soared, swooped, and wheeled, white against an indigo thunder sky. Then came a real canal thrill. I was studying my Ordnance sheet carefully, hoping to get a line on the memorial column to the 'Father of Canals', Francis, Duke of Bridgewater. This rises among some of the finest trees in Britain in Ashridge Park, once his seat, hard by which at Little Gaddesden, he lies in the family vault.

Some 23 years ago when Ashbridge was a Conservative College and I was in my naïve youth, I climbed the monument's many steps and from above the treetops surveyed the plain of Buckinghamshire. Now from the plain I looked up to the treetops five miles distant to see one artificial protuberance among their softer waves, and with a telescope I was able to identify it as the Bridgewater Monument.

We rounded Ivinghoe Beacon without the windings usual at a prominent landmark. Its chalk is scratched unintentionally on the western face to a resemblance to Eros, Achilles, or perhaps one of the 'maidens loth' from Keats's 'Grecian Urn' — her calves revealed by flowing draperies as she turns an apprehensive, or maybe hopeful, head backward over her shoulder. Our intended destination was Cowroast Lock, two miles south of Tring Station, but at Marsworth, having left the Aylesbury arm of the Grand Union on our right, we found that the locks were closed from 8 p.m. to 6 a.m. Our arrival was an hour too late, so we tied up beside 'The White Lion' almost beneath a highly dangerous road bridge on Lower Icknield Way. In the pleasure gardens of the pub, surrounded by a magnificent display of pink peonies, her feet laved in an ornamental pool, was another of Keats's maidens, this time in marble.

What should have been an early night earned on 32 breezy miles with 21 locks, resolved itself into several discussions as soon as our heads touched our pillows, on municipal subsidies for classical music and jazz, precipitated by the boys' gramophone, and the further disposition of the rates. Before we were asleep, a pair of boats chugged past to tie up in first position for locking up in the morning. I missed the name of the motor but the butty was BYFIELD, and the cargo slack coal from Coventry for mills at Hemel

Hempstead. They got away before us as well they were entitled, being working boats, so the first three locks were against us as we rounded Marsworth bend between a field of sickly yellow charlock and the heron-haunted Grand Union reservoirs. But at the fourth lock a British Waterways pair, BARGAS and DUBHE were coming down, their crews eating bacon sandwiches and drinking tea from Coronation mugs at the tillers. So with three favourable locks we were soon chugging along Tring Summit Level in a deep featureless cutting, a three-mile pound unimpeded by wind. It was a calm morning, gleeful with lark-song. We had entered Hertfordshire at Bulbourne on the Upper Icknield Way.

These Marsworth Locks — 'Maffers' to canal folk — have two side-ponds; concrete basins which in time of drought can conserve one side-pond of water on each locking. Coming down, the top side-pond is drawn into the lock in addition to water from the pound above. Then the lock is drained into the bottom side-pond before the bottom gates are opened. This leaves the bottom pond full of water to draw off into the lock for locking up. Thus a pond of water shuttles from upper to lower chamber and in reverse without draining away down the canal. Another shift for conserving water is evident in a notice at Marsworth top lock saying that single boats going down must wait until they can pair up, or until the lock-keeper lets them go.

The side-ponds were not in use at our passage. Their muddy bottoms were bright with buttercups and their walls hung with the delicate lilac flowers of ivy-leaved toadflax. At many of the locks stand large warehouses now in disuse, but the lock cottages are sturdy and of recent date, First World War and thereabouts. Out of the cutting and able to see again, we had a view of the top of the Bridgewater monument on our left. Speed was now restricted by the pair in front of us. Overtaking is taboo, and commercial boats have an obvious priority. Tring was somewhere among the trees and fields away to our right, and near its remote railway station NUTFIELD and COUGHTON were tied up. An Alsatian ran sure-footed along the top-planks and a gipsy-like woman's head, hair ringleted in canal fashion, greeted us from a hatch. There was a goodly collection of boats waiting to descend from

Cowroast, including STENTOR and STIRLING CASTLE, the former belonging to Mr R.H. Lee, Chairman of the Midlands Branch of Inland Waterways Association, the latter the cruising canal liner from Braunston mentioned earlier.

The canal at Cowroast is equidistant between road and rail, and it was far from the fine waterway of yesterday, neither side being shored up or concreted, and the towpath the worst yet from Birmingham, narrow, ragged, and overgrown with grasses and nettles. All that justified my mile walk along it when we locked down, was a fine growth of comfrey. Prolific goat's-beard — Jack-go-to-bed-at-Noon — was not yet awake for the morning.

Berkhamsted came up at 9 a.m. with a St. George's cross flag on its bulky grey church tower, and our progress down the locks through our longest urban area yet excited considerable notice. Residents flocked into back gardens, half-shaved male faces and half-clad female shoulders appeared in windows. We had collected our biggest crowd, including an exciting blonde in red, white, and blue jockey cap, with cherry pyjama trousers, when inevitably came catastrophe. The Rising Sun Inn hung out a strikingly warm glowing sign of some mythological personage driving a chariot with four horses over clouds against a mixture of setting sun and aurora borealis. Performing some manoeuvre with a shaft pole, Ken Guest got it hooked round a flimsy garden fence. Rather than pull this down he loosed the pole and our efforts to retrieve it were much appreciated by a good-humoured audience.

Under way again we found chalk notices on some stanking planks — 'Good luck NORMAN CHAMBERLAIN, Carry on to London'. The 'Stan W' who had signed this was Stan Whitehead, a Boys' Club group leader in Birmingham who has relatives in Berkhamsted. Still our canal ran below the railway, and we were waved on our way by passengers at breakfast on a northbound 'Royal Scot'. Before Bourne End we were running beside watercress beds, and at the swing bridge beside the 'Three Horse Shoes' four young men were working on a splended sacking-covered replica of a camel, obviously a Coronation celebration piece. We had a casualty aboard, Ken Cureton, nursing a broken thumb, the legacy of an argument with a paddle. He left his

windlass on while the ratchet went down and kept his hand in the
way as it whirled madly — by no means an original error.

At Apsley we took on more water. A tall wall ran alongside the
cut with a terraced row of houses across Frogmore Crescent on the
other side, the bedroom windows being at towpath level, and
loyal bunting stretching from them to the wall. Beneath the wall
in the street were a row of what we in Birmingham would call
'brewusses' or brew houses, outhouses for laundering purposes,
usually with boilers. On the outer wall of one of these, down in
the street, was a tap. We slung our hosepipe across the towpath,
over the corrugated roofs but under the streamers, secured it to the
tap and filled up while a woman, whose ear-rings and brooches
with her sombre apparel proclaimed her an ex-canal type, told us
of days when she plied the cut. Another boat appearing, we
untied, sent the lookers-on running with our squirting hose, and
hurried for the open locks.

Industry was now lining the canal: a cask factory; timber yards
with giants of the Chilterns either waiting to be cut up or already
sliced along their lengths and reassembled in their original form
but for thin transverse planks holding them slightly apart; Ashley
paper mills; Nash mills. Narrow boats were more frequent. At
Nash mills we obviously disturbed a pair at Sunday dinner, for on
our appearance at the lock above them they scurried about and got
going to use the favourable locks before we could empty them. On
past Toovey's flour mills and the Ovaltine factory, some beauti-
fully decorated boats being tied alongside with the Ovaltine advert
prominent on their cratches.

This was not an attractive waterway. Road, canal, and railway
run down a valley only a mile or so wide and tree-topped, thus
further restricting the view. Country and town struggle for
mastery with a result creditable to neither. True there was a
Thames Valley atmosphere about Cassiobury Park, Watford,
where the canal more resembles a slow-flowing river, deep among
trees including some giant beeches, and here we had big crowds of
Sunday afternoon strollers. At one of the locks in the park it is said
that boatmen murdered a negro servant detailed by his mistress to
molest boats belonging to the Duke of Bridgewater with whom

she was on unfriendly terms. His ghost now haunts the lockside of evenings and boat families shut their children below on this stretch. We saw no ghost, but passed our first Thames lighter — an authentic barge of 14-ft beam — against a timber yard at Cassio Bridge.

Rickmansworth brought our greatest débâcle. Faced with alternative routes, Paul's indecision landed us with the boat firmly wedged across a blind arm of canal, its rudder on a tree-trunk and roots, its forepeak among some ornamental rockery, and its keel on the mud. Divided counsels as to how we should get off left us with three boys on one bank of the arm faced with a longish walk to join the canal, and one other precariously perched on the rockery, to retrieve whom we had to risk going aground again. Eventually we were all reunited, but during our capers STIRLING CASTLE and STENTOR had caught us. We locked down first at Rickmansworth, and the evening became a race to leave our rivals well behind. This we did, travelling at the best speed I had known in NORMAN CHAMBERLAIN. The canal had become a wide, fairly straight waterway, cutting through a strange country of 'flashes' or meres connected by creeks of still or flowing water. Riverside-type residences sent their lawns to the water's edge, often with cabin cruisers moored alongside. Against these sleek playthings many old timbers were rotting in some of the side pools. Near Uxbridge we glided up to a lock through a number of barges and lighters, one at least with a cargo of Swedish cheese, another with bales of jute heaped against the gunwales. At 9 p.m. we moored at Cowley among a row of converted narrow boats beneath tall trees and opposite a well-patronised pub, our tally for the day 32 miles and 55 locks.

We pampered ourselves on my last morning aboard with a lie-in — until 7 a.m. Shortly thereafter a City-looking gentleman wearing a black homburg and carrying a brief case with which four bottles of milk consorted strangely, picked a nice way among the nettles on the towpath to a cabin cruiser moored at our bows. "Haven't had so many neighbours for a long while," he said.

At 9 a.m. we set off in procession behind STENTOR, a colourful scene which would surely have inspired Handel to some more

'Water Music'. As we were the only boat with a loud hailer, Paul now had a new line in patter for the benefit of the public.

"Inland Waterways Association calling. This is the procession of boats going to the Coronation from all parts of the country, STENTOR and NORMAN CHAMBERLAIN from Birmingham, STORK from Manchester, WAYFARER and WANDERER canal liners, BEATRICE from Paddington, and STIRLING CASTLE from Braunston." STORK was a narrow boat converted into an unsightly conservatory with glass sides. WAYFARER and WANDERER of New-Way Holidays have sailed since 1950 to such places as Newark, Lincoln, Boston, and the Lower Avon Navigation. Each has three single and two double cabins, the current prices for holidays aboard being 9½ guineas single and 8½ guineas double, plus one guinea from July to September. BEATRICE was wallowing in reflected glory. The Coronation Honours announced that morning included a gong for the ex-owner, Peter Scott of Severn Wildfowl Trust. We were second in line, and the diesel boats behind puffed up blue smoke clouds from their exhausts. On the banks the countryside was waving its last flags of elder and hawthorn, with yellow iris, buttercups, and wood avens giving place to that townee flower, ragwort. Near one of many canalside timber yards, at West Drayton Station, we passed the tug LEO with two huge Odell barges.

At West Drayton, Nestlé's factory nods across the water to Kraft cheese. Nearby, several working boats were moored with cargoes of small coal including two Fellows, Morton, & Clayton 'joshers', so called after old Joshua Fellows. A perishing wind was with us. It spread out the Union Jacks on factories effectively, but chilled us to the marrow despite the sun, and it was on a sparkling windswept canal with a stray odour of chocolate in our nostrils from Nestlé's that we tied up at 10.30 a.m. at Bull's Bridge, where 30 or more working boats were awaiting orders. While D.I.W.E. officials inspected our craft, I watched a fascinating microcosm of canal life — a pair of Knill's boats from Braunston breasting up the Paddington arm beneath Bull's Bridge; the blue and yellow of British Waterways; boats of most companies which ply the canal; all gaily bedecked with flags, while as we took the

90 degrees left turn two horse-drawn barges were approaching from Brentford.

The Paddington arm, an inky black channel, led us past enormous timber yards, and where it cleared somewhat there were still many unhappy gudgeon floating belly uppermost. And here were more boats; boats of Thomas Clayton (Paddington) Ltd — MAYFLOWER, ALBERTA, FORGET-ME-NOT; Grand Union Canal Company dredge lighters full of grey muck from the depths; Vokins & Company 'Bens' — BENZIREG, BEN STACK, BEN CRUACHAN, BEN KLIBRESH — a strange mix of Scottish and Yiddish names but all with great sweeping rudders; the lovely greens, reds, and yellows of another Knill pair COLUMBA and LUCY, loveliest boats of the trip; a two-master cabin cruiser LYSANDER; and a Thomas Clayton (Oldbury) narrow boat pulling a lighter the size of Waterloo Bridge.

Northward we went. Some miles ahead Harrow spire rose from its wooded eminence, and Dakota aircraft landed and took off at Northolt. How horribly you pay for the speed by your apprehension in so hostile an element as the air. Gone were the old humpback red canal bridges; in their stead newish concrete structures or great steel girders carrying overcrowded roads westward from London. We passed beneath the railway which, later that day, would carry me back in 2½ hours to Birmingham whence it had taken me over four days to come by canal. The occasional country pub had given place to the frequent factory. Glaxo laboratories had its tricky right hand bend and a trim fringe of Lombardy poplars, followed by a surprising stretch of attractive country only six crowflight miles from Paddington. Then the canal became a River Styx with Charon's long row of cabin cruisers moored alongside Alperton Cemetery. So on, and round Willesden railway junction with its countless coal trucks, and Wormwood Scrubs beyond.

The final mile was fantastic in its revelations of living conditions. Lofty houses rose direct from the canal, their barred lower windows on water level, their first floors looking verandah-fashion through iron rails at the murky cut, washing hanging in the pitifully tiny space over children's toys, other windows rising

yet higher to the ultimate attics, window boxes making a brave
attempt to bring something living into this drab yet fascinating
world. With repartee flung to and fro between our boys and
Cockney kids, we came to our mooring, an unsuspected Venice
behind Paddington Station, and as we rammed home our mooring
stakes two strokes from Big Ben punctuated the hammer-blows.
NORMAN CHAMBERLAIN was dead on time.

Let this chapter end where it began — with the Women's
Training Scheme. Susan Woolfitt gives a graphic description in
Idle Women of the 'bottom road', that *via dolorosa* of boatmen on
the London – Birmingham run. Tyseley or Sampson Road
wharfs attained, and cargoes unloaded, the boats often returned to
one of the mills of Hertfordshire or a Middlesex factory with coals
from the Nuneaton and Coventry mines. To ship this new load
they had to take the dread 'bottom road', a wide loop to the north-
east of Birmingham, joining the Birmingham & Fazeley Canal at
Salford Bridge, and running through Minworth, Fazeley,
Polesworth, Atherstone, and Nuneaton, to rejoin the Grand
Union at Braunston Junction.

Six days after I left NORMAN CHAMBERLAIN in Paddington Basin,
I met her on the return journey at Hatton at 8 o'clock on Sunday
morning, and travelled in to Birmingham getting a glimpse of the
'bottom road' as we dropped down to Salford Bridge where the
boat was to lie for a fortnight giving evening cruises to boys from
north Birmingham clubs. Out in the country the fine Knowle
Locks were immaculate; kingfishers flashed before us, and a flight
of six herons. The next locks were deep in industrial Birmingham
at Bordesley, single ones, their sides as we sank into their noisome
depths shining with black oil down which water ran in globules.
Steadily we dropped, lock after lock, more and more of their
greasy muck finding a way to our silver-gilt deck. At the last lock
before the Adderley Street right turn, the top gate refused to open
sufficiently to let us in. Much prodding with shafts convinced us
that a cast iron pipe, 15 inches in diameter and five feet in length,
similar to others on the towpath, was wedged against the lock-
gate socket. It took nearly 30 minutes to lift one end, hitch a rope
around, and then lift the other end to roll it on to the bank again,

a feat which saved some working boatman with fewer human resources much harder work.

But our troubles were not over. Among scum and flotsam collected in the lock were several stout planks, and we jammed firmly with them pressed against the side. This took another 15 minutes with our shafts, scraping the thick grease from the lockside and plastering it over our hands, clothes and the boat. When finally we broke loose by the combined efforts of a dozen lusty men and youths, my mind went back to the girl boaters, with the butty to bow-haul as well as the motor to manage. I thought too of the canal families who plod this 'bottom road' daily, maybe on short local hauls, the women and children pulling the butty with ropes oozing filthy oil and black mud, with soot and smoke and the reek of the gasworks in their dilated nostrils.

This was the other side of the canal picture — a far cry from the idyllic leisurely progress between banks of hawthorn and fields of buttercups with good fresh air around, and far country horizons to behold.

CHAPTER SIX

I find a crib in the hayloft of the butty KUBINA,
*and cruise by Thomas Telford's embankments
and cuttings up the 'Shroppy' to the Manchester
Ship Canal.*

There are many obvious disadvantages in life on the canals, but at Yates's Boatyard, Norton Canes, where spoil from the southern fringes of Cannock coalfield renders the landscape sterile but for the banks of hairy willow herb which mark the line of the cut, I saw one of its advantages. When we house-dwellers repair and renovate our homes we live among the resultant chaos. But when the Berridge family had their home redecorated, they just left it in the hands of the repair party and moved to another for as long as the operation lasted.

Or rather, half their home. For Leslie Berridge, his wife, and their six children ranging from 15-year-old Annie to 15-month-old Linda, live in motor-boat TOWY and its butty KUBINA, and only the latter was at Yates's. The Berridge goods and chattels were just transferred to a 'change-boat' — TIBER by name — and this strange confluence of Welsh and Italian rivers continued to ply the Shropshire Union Canal until KUBINA was again house-worthy. And it was at Norton Canes one July morning that I watched the Berridges take over their own butty again, resplendent from colourful tiller-post to the red, blue, and yellow discs on the bend of the forepeak, which distinguish a boat belonging to Thomas Clayton (Oldbury) Ltd. Yates's own boats, usually let out to carriers of coal from the Cannock pits to Birmingham, are marked with three diamonds.

At some future date I was to travel with the hospitable Berridges from Oldbury to Ellesmere Port, and had driven to Norton Canes to make final arrangements with the skipper. Immediately I found the solution to my accommodation problems, for I should be two or three nights aboard. Narrow boats retain two relics of horse-drawn days. A barrel, in KUBINA's case painted green with black bands and standing aft of the towing mast, used to function as corn bin. Now it is a repository for coils of rope and other impedimenta. In addition, hay was kept in the forepeak, and in the 'hayloft' as it is called, I saw an ideal berth in which to instal myself without upsetting the family sleeping plan. This is — Mr and Mrs Berridge in the cross bed which falls across the width of KUBINA's cabin, with Linda, Johnie aged six, and Tommie, aged four, deployed elsewhere in the cabin. Annie, and Gertie, 14, have the cross bed in TOWY, sharing their cabin with 10-year-old Leslie, who is allowed to remain their room-mate until he is 14, when regulations say he must be moved from the girls.

Mr Berridge consenting to my suggestion, I presented myself on Tuesday, August 18th, with a couple of small mattresses once

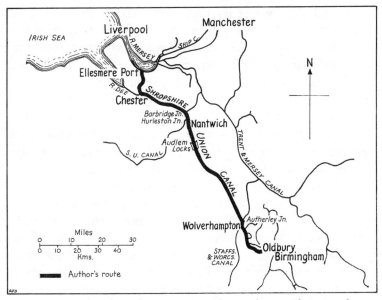

8: The Shropshire Union and Manchester Ship Canals

used in my twins' cots, and a further legacy of their extreme youth in the form of a domestic utensil indispensable on a boat without indoor sanitation. The mattresses fitted on two planks fixed athwartships, and I should lie against a bulkhead separating the hayloft from the oil holds. For TOWY and KUBINA were on the diesel oil run, on which Clayton's boats carry 2000 tons monthly from the Manchester Ship Canal to the Shell Mex tanks at Langley Green, Staffordshire, whence it is distributed for furnaces throughout the Midlands. I could not stand upright in my 'cabin' unless I did so with head and shoulders protruding from the hatch, which had a slide cover brightly decorated with a red club on a white pattern against a green background. The timbers around me curved to the interior shape of the forepeak, and, all in all, it was as snug a billet as heart could desire. But KUBINA had done several journeys since her face-lift, and a little oil, with a lot of smell, had seeped through into the hayloft. Assured that diesel oil fumes are not dangerous, I settled in happily.

I had been warned to be at the starting point, Junction Wharf, Oldbury, by 11 a.m. Les, it seemed, had some business at that hour, and then we could begin our journey of 77 miles to Ellesmere Port. The business turned out to be nothing other than a visit from his insurance agent to collect weekly premiums, and this gentleman told me he had a number of policy-holders among the floating population at the wharf, though I forgot to ask if a canal child is regarded as a special risk with increased premium or reduced benefit.

Business disposed of — with a few half-hearted coughs and splutters TOWY's engine tuned in to a steady throb, and we were off into the milky cut, KUBINA close-hauled, her nose held against TOWY's stern fender by two rope couplings looped between the red stud of the butty and two 'dollies' on TOWY's after deck. It was a sporting gymnastic exercise to move from one boat to another, and though I soon achieved competence, my figure precluded any grace in the achievement. My first shock was a speedy realisation that the vibration on TOWY made the notes I tried to write almost illegible, and I soon recalled from my acquaintance with her 15 months earlier that the exhaust fumes spurt from the engine room only some six feet from the steerer's eyes. Add to this the acrid smoke from the stove chimney even nearer, and the man at the tiller has a tough time. Fortunately, fire for cooking was confined to the butty so we were spared that affliction as I stood with Les watching old familiar landmarks glide past.

Annie had not come aboard yet, but was trudging the towpath with a large bundle of washing slung in a sheet over her back. This she delivered to one of the Berridge clan who lives at a canal-side cottage, to be laundered and collected on the boat's return. Then, at the next bridge hole she came aboard. The girls are very like their mother, slim, and with lank black hair, though Mrs Berridge's face is burned a deeper, almost gypsy brown.

The pair of family boats constitutes the aristocracy of the canal world, which is not without its lower strata as we were soon to see. Passing a chap in a mouldy green trilby, baling water out of the bowels of an open boat, we came up to a small pontoon which Les recognised as one he had once given a tow. Its owners were a bearded young man in rosy slacks and a blonde girl wearing green jeans, seemingly arty types who prefer to sleep beneath a tarpaulin slung over their open boat rather than grapple with the problem of more orthodox housing. These ex-Army pontoons are popular for conversion into cabin cruisers. When given the shape of a boat they can be attractive, but too often they retain their two blunt ends and look for all the world like the top deck of a submerged bus.

Leaving Brades Lock on the right I entered a canal which was new to me. There are three main levels on the Birmingham canal system, all connected by locks. We were travelling on the highest of these, the Wolverhampton level, of which there are 54 miles at 473 feet. The Birmingham level of 33 miles is 20 feet lower, while the Walsall level of 20 miles is 408 feet above sea level. Soon we were crossing an aqueduct above the Birmingham level with the portal of Netherton tunnel about 100 yards below and to our left. On past a disused basin from which Les had taken many loads of bedsteads to London; alongside grey slag overgrown with the yellow of ragwort and the purple of willow herb; wide views below and around of the vast conurbation of the Black Country, its electricity stations with huge bobbins of cooling towers most prominent of all features. And, lord over the scene long before these arose, the jagged walls of Dudley Castle rose above the waves of their surrounding trees.

Tipton gave us among other things an octagonal toll house, no longer used, and a bomb ruin on the outside of a bend which looked like the result of some bad steering on the cut. Beneath Owen Street bridge on a graceful curve, only a wall kept the canal out of Tipton's main thoroughfare. Coseley tunnel, 300 yards long, provided a remarkable phenomenon. A stiff breeze was blowing through against us, carrying a veritable snowstorm of 'angels' from seeding willow herb, and we came out festooned and bearded with white down. The tunnel is a wide one with a good railed towpath. Just beyond it a tug chugged past us with a train of four coal boats.

Having previously travelled on TOWY singly, I was now with a pair in action for the first time, a combined 140 feet of two tar boats. The decks were of transverse wooden planks with occasional hatch covers. Three coils of rope lay at intervals along TOWY's length; a broom, the bike for lock-wheeling leaning against the cabin. Synchronising with the beat of the engine, spurts of blue smoke leapt from the exhaust. A mop handle was propped on a colourful water can — painted by Les himself. Beside the black cabin stove chimney with its three polished brass rings, Les leaned lightly on the tiller smoking one of his home-rolled cigarettes, and wearing a cloth cap and blue overalls beneath his jacket. Now and then, swinging out of alignment, KUBINA came in view, newly painted above the black hull in ochrous hue; her mast diamonded in blue, red, white, and yellow; green corn bin, brown cabin, and Mrs Berridge bare-headed at the wooden tiller.

So we passed Mill Hole, Wolverhampton, where the blue and yellow was much in evidence, it being a British Waterways depot. More colourful, Clayton's LEAM passed us, horse-drawn, and Mrs Berridge exchanged a sentence with her sister who lives on LEAM. Written beneath one bridge was the supplication 'Please Refrain from Chalking Rude Words.' the next was dated 1879 and

14: Bearley Aqueduct on the Stratford-on-Avon Canal

15: Western portal of Brandwood Tunnel, Stratford-on-Avon Canal

16: NORMAN CHAMBERLAIN near Lifford Paper Mill

17: Mooring NORMAN CHAMBERLAIN after dark near Warwick

18: An athletic way of getting ashore from NORMAN CHAMBERLAIN

19: Eating arrangements on NORMAN CHAMBERLAIN

20: NORMAN CHAMBERLAIN meets the Inland Waterway Cruising Company's NELSON and NANCY near Leamington

21: Leslie Berridge (left) steers TOWY and KUBINA breasted up on the Manchester Ship Canal

22: Two Clayton pairs awaiting loading with diesel at Stanlow (©
Birmingham Weekly Post)

23: The Newark cut

24: TEES passing Newark Castle (© Waterways Museum, Stoke Bruerne)

25: Torksey Lock, junction of the Foss Dyke and the Trent

26: TEES towing two dumb barges (© Birmingham Weekly Post)

27: Leaving TEES in Hull's Old Harbour for an evening in The Land of Green Ginger (author in cap)

inscribed *E Tenebris Oritur Lux*, Wolverhampton's civic motto. On 31 December 1898 this was changed to the English 'Out of Darkness Cometh Light', but Latin or English it remains the same to the normally illiterate boatmen. We were now at the top of the Wolverhampton 21, the top lock being at Little's Lane Bridge.

This was my first experience of locking with a pair of boats. As the locks are single, motor and butty cannot breast up so must go down separately. Normally a horse is hired to pull the butty, but none was available. Two characters who seemed aware of this had joined us, and they set about 'bow-hauling' KUBINA down the locks, helped occasionally by the girls and me, though Gertie and Annie were busy with windlasses, drawing the sluices and opening and shutting the lock gates. The younger of our haulers was a taciturn type whose invariable reply to any remark from the girls was 'Shut yer phizog'. When a horse is used, the account goes to the Oldbury office. When bow-hauling is necessary, Les is allowed six shillings and nine pence, but as it costs seven shillings to hire the haulers he loses on the transaction. He can remember the time when men fought to take the boat up and down for two shillings and six pence.

There was material for the modern symphonist in our bow-haul down the Wolverhampton 21 — the rattle of the paddle ratchets, the hollow thud as our empty boat hit the lock gates and the crash as the gates closed behind us, the swish and rush of water, the prolonged roar of trains over steel bridges and stone arches, the steady crunch of feet on gravel, and a theme from the Volga Boatman, sung by workers sunning themselves through the iron railings, as they must have sung it many dinner times to boats bow-hauling past.

We were two hours in the locks; two hours which brought transition from town to country, for the last few pounds ran alongside Dunstall Park race-course, a wide arena of bright green fringed by trees and overlooked by an enormous arched railway viaduct. The canal makes a splendid grandstand, but, said Annie "Two cut-gaffers turn us off if we stop to watch the races — they're only here theirselves when the races are on." Blackberry pickers were now busy on the bank, and way back, St. Peter's four-pinnacled tower bade us farewell from Wolverhampton.

In the bottom pound there was a passing encounter with two more of Clayton's River class boats, USK and TAY, homeward bound with their butties, all full of oil and low in the water. The Wolverhampton locks are the typical narrow locks — single top gate and double at the bottom, all except No 20, which for some reason has both gates single. At Lock 21, beneath a bridge with an elaborate wrought-iron lamp bracket silhouetted against the sky, we joined the Staffordshire & Worcestershire Canal at Aldersley Junction — a real canal collector's piece. A tall red-brick toll house rises either side of the junction, and a yellow finger post (the term is used in preference to 'sign post' in the Black Country) points back to Wolverhampton, left to Stourport and the Severn, and right to Autherley Junction.

We awaited TOWY at the bottom lock, and as she passed, Les deftly slipped a loop over our stud and, together again, we went under Aldersley Bridge, No 64, which has a picturesque separate little arch for the towpath. Autherley Junction is less than a mile north of Aldersley, and there we branched left on the main line of the Shropshire Union Canal, entering it beneath the junction bridge which is marked No 1 — bridges are numbered along canals from the last junction.

These two junctions are interesting illustrations of canal politics. The Staffordshire & Worcestershire is the oldest of the three canals involved, and when, in 1768, the Birmingham Canal was authorised, Langford, the Birmingham historian, has written: 'on receiving the agreeable news that His Majesty had been at the House of Peers and signed the Bill for making the Navigable Canal from this town (Birmingham) to Wolverhampton, the bells were set to ringing which were continued the whole day.' This popular canal was the first to be completed as a tributary to an already existing canal, and the pound of flesh exacted by the Staffordshire & Worcestershire was the lock of water which comes down with every boat passing from the newer to the older canal, consequently there is no stop lock at Aldersley Junction to retain the Birmingham Canal's water. But for every boat passing from the Birmingham to the Shropshire Union and vice versa, via the Staffordshire & Worcestershire, the Shropshire Union is entitled to a share in the lock of water received at Aldersley. This it takes at a special sluice and paddle which by-passes Autherley stop-lock.'

The Shropshire Union Canal was formed in the mid-1840s by the amalgamation of the Ellesmere & Chester Canal, the Birmingham & Liverpool Junction, the Shrewsbury, and two parts of the Montgomeryshire Canal. The intention of the company, in which two railways were empowered to become stockholders, was to convert part of the canal to railways and to construct certain new railways. In 1847 the London & North Western Railway became lessee of the entire system, which received a respite and was encouraged to accept commercial loads because it ran over some areas not covered by railways. When the Manchester Ship Canal was opened in 1894, Ellesmere Port, the outlet for the Shropshire Union on the Mersey, enhanced its status, and the railway decided to work the canal as a supplement to its system. It not only constructed a barge dock, quays, and warehouses costing over £250,000 at Ellesmere Port, but set up as a canal carrier itself — practically the only case of a railway doing so.

The section of the 'Shroppy' on which we were now travelling was the Birmingham & Liverpool Junction, authorised in 1826 to reduce the distance and lockage between Birmingham and Liverpool to 94 miles with 69 locks, as against 114 miles and 99 locks via the Trent & Mersey Canal. Generally, the coming of railways sounded the death knell of the golden era of canals, but since those days man has conquered another element — with what mortal danger to himself — and to our right grounded aircraft glistened in the sun on Wolverhampton Municipal Airport as we moved out of Autherley towards the Boulton-Paul aircraft works. Far beyond, across the valley of the Penk, was the dark horizon of Cannock Chase, always sombre-looking, while over the hedge on our left potato pickers were busy in the fields.

It was turning out an expansive afternoon, with a bounding breeze from the north-west, a benign sun, and tumbled cumulo-stratus cloud. Already, far inland though we were, seagulls were flying along the line of the canal, and peewits hurried about the stubble and gambolled in the wind. Golden domes of wheat-fields alternated with the shining green of sugar beet, and as we approached Brewood the canal narrowed, while larch and silver birch bordered either bank. This was a foretaste of the deep narrow cuttings which alternate with long stretches of broader canal high on embankments. Just short of Brewood an ornamental balustered bridge carried the drive to Chillington Hall across the canal, and as we emerged from the cutting into the open again Brewood was visible to our right across a meadow where black and white Friesian cattle matched a magpie cottage or two before the red row of houses sloped up to the church spire.

Barely more than a mile and we were crossing Watling Street, high on Telford's fine aqueduct, dated 1832, with the Aqueduct Inn beside it. Nearby, a canal mile post read Autherley 6, Nantwich 33. With only about 20 miles behind us we were having an early night, and in two miles more we tied up at Wheaton Aston lock around 6.30 p.m. Here, the first job was a counting of heads to make sure the six children were all present and correct. The wear and tear on Mrs Berridge's nerves is considerable, and from time to time, not having noticed one of the children for a while, she would shout an enquiry until he turned up from somewhere. Myself excepted, there was not a swimmer aboard. But Les is a past master at fishing young Leslie out of the cut on a boathook, though there was the occasion when, encased in plaster because of a back injury, he got there only just in time to prevent the boy drowning. Little Linda sits happily, and as yet safely, in KUBINA's tiny enclosed after deck.

Our companions for the night, tied up before us, were the Walters family aboard Clayton's RIBBLE and FORTH. In addition to their complement of small children, they had on their decks a diminutive hen coop with a couple of Plymouth Rocks, and a dog kennel with a nondescript mongrel.

Throughout the day there had been incessant cups of tea on our boats, made with the tinned milk on which the Berridge's largely rely. Hunks of bread and cheese had sustained us after the tussle with Wolverhampton locks, and there was an evening meal of bacon and beans eaten on the cabin roof in the cheerful glow of a westering sun. A mile or so to eastward of the canal this lit up the solid square tower of Lapley Church so invitingly that I set out to inspect it. Across fields I tramped, among the stubble of recently-stooked barley, through bracken neck high, over green pastures with lengthening shadows to the crunching of cows as they cropped the grass. Once a whirring covey of partridges erupted from the corn, and I came at last, after a stern jaunt across country, to winding lanes which took me through the village to its church. From the porch I looked back over much of Staffordshire and all Shropshire, stretched towards the sunset with the Wrekin dark and prominent. The even upland skyline of Cannock Chase closed the east behind the church.

Lapley church is a building of mystery and might-have-been. Luckily the vicar was sitting in the nave and he explained the many noteworthy features, though I was able to draw his attention to an inscription on a buttress at the north of the massive central tower which he knew only in an identical position on the south. This was the date 1637 with the names Edward Berree and William Tonck, cut roughly in the stone, the R being missing from Edward on the south side. There was no doubt that this tower had at one time been supported by transepts, for its width was as great as the body of the church. At the 'crossing' the remaining west arch is Norman and the east Gothic, both restored. The chancel, of equal length with the nave and not raised above it, was a weeping chancel, inclined to the south sufficiently to make it difficult for worshippers in the south of the nave to see the altar. The weeping chancels are said to commemorate the drooping of Christ's head on the cross — further evidence that the church was once cruciform.

A very new and colourless east window is the church's only unattractive feature. Beneath it, within the altar rail, is a fine stone under which was buried a priest who might have been John de Derleston. Also near the altar are remains of a tessellated floor, and, in the south wall of the chancel which is otherwise re-remarkably bare, there protrudes a finely carved Flemish door, the origin of which was unknown to the vicar. There is, however, a

Dutch font, carved with Biblical scenes and inscribed 'Het Geborte Christi' beneath the representation of the birth of Christ. Again, no one knows whence this font came originally, though its carvings proclaim it eleventh or twelfth century. Probably thrown out of the church by the Cromwellians, it was found a hundred years ago doing duty as a drinking trough in a farmyard, and restored to its rightful position on a modern shaft and base.

From outside, several small Norman arches can be detected in the fabric, one springing from the roof of the nave on the western base of the tower. In the vicar's words the church is of 'utterly higgledy-piggledy architecture'. Since my return home after reaching Ellesmere Port, the vicar (Rev. G.B.J.R. Watson, M.A.) has sent me the following account of the church's foundation:

'In the year 1061, Aldred, Archbishop of York, went on a pilgrimage to Rome, taking with him many noble Englishmen, amongst whom was Burchard, youngest son of Algar, Earl of Mercia, and a grandson of Lady Godiva. Returning from Rome by way of Rheims, Burchard became mortally ill and was nursed by the monks of St. Remigius at Rheims. Before his death he requested that he should be buried in the abbey at Rheims, promising in return that certain lands centred around Lapley should be given to the monastery. Earl Algar, with the consent of Edward the Confessor, fulfilled his dying son's promise. Accordingly about the year 1063, Benedictine monks from the abbey of St. Remigius formed a cell at Lapley and built a church and priory. The Abbots of Rheims, through their representatives the Priors of Lapley, became Lords of the Manor, which they held until the dissolution of alien priories by Henry V in 1414, when the lands and property were transferred to an English college at Tonge. After 1414, therefore, the church became the parish church of Lapley.'

I left the church to the clangour of its bells as the ringers put in some practice. The sun, well round to right of the Wrekin, was sinking into an ominous cloudbank with an equally evil canopy of blue-black stratus clouds above. By the time I reached the boats there was a clear amber sky in the west and the inky stratus had turned grey, with orange and red wisps in the zenith, and there were two moons, both gibbous, one in the sky, the other in the cut.

The Berridges have a battery wireless set in KUBINA's cabin, and they had collected a newly-charged accumulator from the garage at Wheaton Aston and were enjoying some music prior to a final hour at the Hartley Arms. There, débâcle overtook me. Although I have never played darts, Les encouraged me to give him several games, and though defeated I was not dishonoured. Then another boatman took him on and I was given the job of keeping score. This necessitated subtracting the players' initial scores from 301, and continuing to subtract successive scores from the remainder. Painfully I bent to my task, helped by the chalk and blackboard. The boatmen, with whom education is not considered a strong suit, regarded the 'writing gentleman' with astonishment, and proceeded to do his arithmetic for him in their heads in the twinkling of an eye. This, I am told, is an automatic accomplishment of all darts players, but I had the grace to feel somewhat ashamed.

Leaving them to it, and Mrs Berridge to a nice cosy chat with Mrs Walters over a couple of glasses of stout, I picked my way back to the boats by the light of the torch which was my sole illumination in the hayloft as I struggled into my pyjamas, pulled trousers, socks, and pullover above them, and resigned myself to a sleepless night in my two blankets. My fears were realised, and the melancholy tremolo of the owls gave place to early cock-crow before I contrived an hour's slumber.

The square of starry sky seen through my hatch slide had become pearly grey when I was wakened by sleepy shouts for Sam, and the knocking of a cabin wall between FORTH and RIBBLE. Simultaneously, dull thuds and rumblings, and a buoyancy about KUBINA showed that Les was astir. Though it was not quite 5 a.m. I was not sorry to get up. No amount of experience in beds other than my own overcomes my inability to sleep anywhere but on my domestic couch. There was mist on the water and a suspicion of sunshine. After several splutters RIBBLE's engine took up a steady beat and they were off. More spluttering astern and TOWY crept slowly forward, Les handing me a cup of tea as he passed, and coupling up. We too were off — a big day of nearly 50 miles before us.

A golden sun had come up over Cannock Chase, and its rays, slanting from beneath mother-of-pearl cloudlets, threw long shadows from tree and hedgerow on the low sea of mist covering the pastures until it looked like ice-bound flood water. So dense was the mist, and so even, that only the tops of the corn stooks were visible above it. In a cutting tall ashes thrust their topmost branches into the sunlight. Then Les gave me the tiller, and with instructions to slow down two boats' lengths before the frequent accommodation bridges, he went astern, leaving me sole custodian of TOWY, though Annie and Gertie were still sleeping in the cabin below me. I was really on my mettle. TOWY responded better and more quickly to her tiller than NORMAN CHAMBERLAIN, and KUBINA did not complicate matters at all. Nevertheless I thanked Telford for his straight cut, for, while I treat NORMAN CHAMBERLAIN with every respect, I was now in charge not of a plaything, but of the home of eight people, and though the bridges were fine structures of grey stone they were rather deceptive, the towpath jutting well into the cut.

But all went well. How much better to steer one's way along a lonely canal at 4 m.p.h. than to hurtle among traffic in a car at 60. Especially when the leisurely journey is punctuated by the flash of three kingfishers.

Gnosall has a deep cutting where ash and sycamore meet overhead to form a tunnel of greenery, and a more authentic tunnel, 100 yards long, cut through the red sandstone, its walls jagged, natural, and unbricked. It also has a ghost. Georgina Jackson's collection of Shropshire folklore tells us that on January 21st, 1879, a labourer carrying luggage from Ranton to Newport was attacked at the canal bridge at Gnosall by a black creature with great white eyes which the policeman readily identified as the ghostly 'man-monkey' said to haunt the spot since a man was drowned in the canal there.

Imaginations might well run rife at Gnosall however, what with the Boat Inn at one bridge and the 'Navigation' at the next, only 300 yards away. The 'Boat' has an unusual curved white wall, well matched by its curved white windows. Some pleasure craft were moored at Gnosall, and in one a boy in pyjamas waved from his bunk.

We cruised out of Gnosall above the Norbury valley on an embankment about a mile long with stop locks at each end to impound the waters should a breach occur. The stop planks, a familiar canal feature which are normally used for this purpose, have been protected in the past on the Shropshire Union by ridged wooden shelters. These are accessible to mischievous boys, so now padlocked concrete lockers are replacing them.

At Norbury Junction, where there is a maintenance depot, the Newport Canal branched to the left for its pleasant four miles across Shropshire pastures to Newport, whence it continues south-west to join up with the old Shropshire tub-boat canals around Oakengates and Wellington. Traffic no longer uses the Newport branch from Norbury, and the top lock, just behind the white junction bridge, has been converted into a dry dock. Mrs Berridge used to travel the branch frequently, and Clayton boats have fetched tar from Newport gasworks, but the canal was so shallow that only 15 tons could be carried instead of 22 tons, and the journey was no longer an economic proposition.

Another of the now familiar narrow cuttings carried us, at the Eccleshall road bridge, beneath the shortest telegraph pole on the Shropshire Union. Telegraph wires run along the towpath and are enabled to zigzag beneath the lofty arch of this bridge by the construction of a second lower arch on which stands just the crosstrees of a telegraph pole. Having seen this wonder, I went aft with Les for breakfast of bacon and tomatoes while Mrs Berridge took over the steering. While eating, I had my first feel of the butty tiller, the familiar length of wood painted red, blue, and yellow. The general principle was to try and keep in a straight line with the motor-boat, which meant the normal technique of steering, rendered rather easier because the motor, in good hands, was already keeping the butty's nose in mid-canal.

As yet none of the children had put in an appearance. "Ain't it Heaven with 'em all in bed," said Les in heartfelt tones, and I concurred as heartily, for what with NORMAN CHAMBERLAIN too, my boats had always suffered a surfeit of youngsters. While we breakfasted, the square tower of High Offley church came into view on a hill a mile or so to our right, and soon we had a first glimpse of Cadbury's Knighton factory. Les was back on TOWY by the time we chugged beneath the cover at the factory wharf, and I caught sight of hundreds of milk churns on a loading bay back in the factory. I was enjoying the morning sunshine on the nose of KUBINA while Les contentedly whistled 'Back to Sorrento' as he directed us along the cut. Across a cornfield, contrasting with our straight course, I watched a snipe jinking like a rugger three-quarter side-stepping his opponents.

After a morning walk along the towpath north of Knighton, I perched astride TOWY's nose, the red stud sticking in my stomach, and my shadow thrown before me as we travelled through plains and ploughlands where I was glad to see conical stooks rather than oblong bales which bespeak mechanical harvesting. Young swallows were flocking on the telegraph wires — and greenfinches. Substantial red farms glided past, and all the time distance was ticking off slowly but surely, a milepost proclaiming Autherley 22 miles back and Nantwich 17 ahead. We overtook a butty full of gravel towed by a little grey tug which obligingly let us through as the canal narrowed to Drayton Rocking, where it runs more like a well-maintained ditch than a canal between walls of red sandstone, shored up in places to prevent landslips. It was in this cutting that I saw, most unexpectedly, one plant of yellow centaury.

There was a period of activity at Tyrley five locks where we bow-hauled down after filling our two water cans from a tap on a slippery slope in a spinney. Market Drayton church tower, scene of the climbing exploits of the youthful Clive of India, was now peeping at us from the trees on the left, but we saw little enough of the town. The three boys were sprawled on KUBINA's deck, Leslie day-dreaming while Johnnie fished abortively for tiddlers and allowed water and mud to drip on the back of the unsuspecting Tommie as he explored his net after each cast. The skipper looked up from the cabin to remark that they were playing 'this cricket' already, and on my telling him that the fifth test would last six days if necessary, he observed that it sounded a particularly stupid game. One advantage of canal travel is that you can keep cricket at arm's length.

For my diversion there were the hundreds of small fishes stranded and slithering desperately on the mud as our passage sucked the water from them momentarily, only to overwhelm them a moment later with a tidal wave. There were, too, the flowers — the lilac puff-balls of water mint, blue skull cap, purple of hairy willow herb and knapweed, red drupes of the guelder rose, scabious, St. John's wort, sneezewort, yarrow, and a great thrill — a patch of yellow loosestrife. Some reed mace thrust up from the bank at one spot, and beyond Nantwich corn marigold and moneywort, the creeping Jenny of our gardens, were to become common. One wild plant is known to the Berridge girls — comfrey, the leaves of which they gather for their grandfather to make an infusion for the treatment of his bad leg. Blackberries were prolific, and new hazel nuts forming. Les tried to point out to me the little water bird called the 'jackdowker' by canal folk, but it remained unidentified. It could not have been the moorhen, for he knew that by name, and was surprised to learn that I have never eaten it. Cooked in fat it is like chicken, and is best caught at night when blinded by the light of a torch in its haunts on overhanging branches near water level. And I was shown the spot, near Market Drayton, where once the canal 'bosted' causing TOWY to turn back to Autherley and take the Staffordshire & Worcestershire Canal to the Potteries and so via the Middlewich branch back to the Shropshire Union.

On through Adderley Locks, and so down to the Audlem 15. Usually there is a horse to be hired for the butty, but like the one at Wolverhampton, he wasn't available. So we bow-hauled down. As an aid to slimming I commend bow-hauling to any woman who covets the sylph-like figure usual in a woman of the canals. It's about as likely to kill as any other method of reducing, but if she survives she'll have a figure like a strip of pump water, and men will find her the less attractive in consequence.

To add to our privations on the Audlem 15, it began to rain at the top lock. So I set about the task wearing raincoat and hat in addition to being well clothed beneath. We went first with the butty, leaving Les to work TOWY down on his own. Ahead were RIBBLE and FORTH, and Gertie was filling the locks for us as they emptied them. This left Mrs Berridge at KUBINA's tiller, and Annie and me with the towrope, and after one or two locks we evolved the best system. Unless it is coiled expertly as the butty loses way in each lock, the towrope can become no end of a nuisance. So, because I just could not coil it, Annie did so while I crossed the bottom lock gates and drew the outside paddle. To hands and arms unaccustomed to using a windlass this is no picnic in itself. KUBINA now being in the lock, and the top gate shut in that deft fashion of looping the stern rope over the gate post and letting the boat's momentum close it, Annie was free to draw the paddle on the inside (or the towpath side). Not relishing a crossing of the lock gate above the cauldron of water now boiling up below, I would cross by way of KUBINA's deck while she was still high in the lock, and, taking up the neatly coiled rope off the balance beam, would go forward, waiting for Annie to open the gates. Then, with the rope over my shoulder, I strained forward, and slowly the boat came out into the pound. Bent nearly double I hauled the butty forward for two or three hundred yards, helped towards the next lock by Annie, who had stayed behind to close the paddles of the last gate.

So it went on, over 14 pounds and 15 locks. The rope became wet and gritty. Soon my raincoat was so sodden as to be no further use, so I shed it and my jacket, hauling in my shirt, wet by rain outside and by sweat within. For 90 minutes this went on, but below the bottom lock I forgot my discomfort at a winding pool with the finest flowering plants of arrowhead I have ever seen, and some good clumps of water plantain. We rested for a few minutes while Mrs Berridge went into Audlem shopping, and the church clock — another typical square tower — struck three.

We were now in Cheshire, and, in another mile, at the aqueduct across the River Duckow, we ran off my Stafford O.S. sheet. For the next dozen or so miles I was without a map — a fish out of water. If I had to name the greatest friend I have found in feature journalism I should say the one inch Ordnance map.

At Agg Green we dropped down the last two narrow locks on the Shropshire Union, so, with this impediment removed, wider boats can get up to Nantwich with its capacious and well-kept basin. We skirted round the west of this Cheshire salt town, crossing another aqueduct beside a big school and the cottage hospital. For a while the canal forgot it was made by Telford and indulged in several uncharacteristic bends, on which were a number of anglers among whom elderly women predominated.

The rain had ceased, but it was a dull depressing afternoon as we left behind us the junction of the beautiful Llangollen Canal at Hurleston. Five locks raise it from the Shropshire Union, locks too narrow, Les told me, for the normal narrow boat, a fact I was able to check next day when, returning to Birmingham by car, I had an unexpected encounter with STIRLING CASTLE at Chester. Pleasure cruising from Braunston, she had tried to enter the Llangollen Canal but proved too wide for the locks. The boats used on the Llangollen were known as 'trench boats'.

At Wettenhall we shot the hundredth bridge from Autherley, and soon the canal was spanned by a roof at the warehouse built by the old Shropshire Union, a warehouse with arcaded sides and a rickety wooden footbridge high above the canal. Here, too, was the branch which ran by four locks in eleven miles to Middlewich, the usual route of British Waterways boats from Wolverhampton on their regular run via the Weaver Navigation to Weston Point and Runcorn.

A thoroughly dismal evening had set in with heavy rain against which Les merely turned up his jacket collar and hunched his shoulders. My gloom was dispelled somewhat when we ran on to my Chester O.S. sheet at Calveley, and at Bunbury we breasted up, i.e. tied TOWY and KUBINA side by side with ropes at nose and stern to descend our first double lock. Bunbury lock is double in two senses. It is wide enough to take two boats, and it has a double chamber: really two separate locks, where the bottom gate of the higher is the top gate of the lower.

This Cheshire countryside was tumbled and hillocky, with

alders lining the canal. We had decided to tie up for the night at
Beeston, and from Tilstone Lock the castle could be seen on its
towering tree-skirted crag — seen but not distinguished from the
rock, with the yellow murk of a windy rainy sunset behind it. One
more lock, the Iron Lock, so called because it has iron sides,
another at Beeston itself, and we were gliding to a tie-up in the
reeds behind 'The Royal Oak'. "They've got television and we
stand in the passage and watch the pictures" said Annie, who also
told me that she likes the Oldbury tie-up because she gets a night
at the cinema. Throughout the journey Annie, who was my
closest friend — Gertie being fully occupied with one of the boys
aboard RIBBLE — referred to me, as did the others, as 'the master'.
This was no reflection on my status; it was merely in lieu of 'Mr
Bird', and my photographer colleague, John Turnbull, who cut us
off by car here and there, was 'the other master'.

Just across the canal from our mooring was Beeston and
Tarporley Station on the main line to North Wales. What
memories this brought back of childhood holidays at Rhyl, when
the sight of Beeston's spectacular rock crowned by its castle was
one of the major events of the train ride. I found myself becoming
almost maudlin in the dank gloom as I looked down 35 years
across the darkening countryside and wondered if any of our adult
pleasures can match those of childhood. I put such stupid thoughts
resolutely behind me when I realised that we were spending the
night in sight of two castles, for Peckforton on its wooded hills
had swum out from behind Beeston's pile. We saw only the
obvious in those days — I never remember noticing Peckforton
castle and its pleasant little range, though they are much more
attractive than their obtrusive neighbour.

In the gusty dusk I had seen what I took to be an echelon of
curlews flying determinedly north. As more and more followed I
felt convinced that they were gulls, though I could not give them
a name. There was no doubt that the seabirds flying restlessly up
and down the canal were black-headed gulls, and against a
momentary window of pellucid afterglow in the stormy west, a
wide-winged heron planed into a nearby meadow. Then grey
ragged clouds drifted up, and more rain. As I lay down to a rather

better sleep than the previous night, there was a swishing in the rushes and a lapping of the wind-ruffled water outside my cosy retreat.

Thursday's reveille was almost a repetition of the previous day — the coming to life of KUBINA on her unstable element as Les moved about aft, followed by the clump of his feet along the deck and "Are you awake, Nellie?" to Mrs Walters aboard FORTH. Seemingly she was, for there came the usual splutter of a reluctant engine, a few coughs, and the regular chug. They were away. Then I heard TOWY scraping alongside, and, thrusting a bleary-eyed and tousled head out of my hatch-slide I was not disappointed. Les was gliding up, in one hand my morning tea, the other ready to grab the coupling rope.

By the time I was dressed I could look back on the Peckforton Hills in the early morning light with their monstrous outlier, Beeston crag, to left of them. An inviting range they made; a mixture of fields, woody knolls, fretted tree-lines on their crests, and sheltered hollows. One particularly entrancing hill had a steady dip slope of chequered fields rising to a sharp point above a well-wooded escarpment. The weather, which had not been so bad in the night as was anticipated, still looked a doubtful quantity, though most of the cloud was to leeward. I clambered aboard TOWY, hoping that Les would go aft on a similar errand to the previous morning, leaving me with the tiller. He divined my hopes — and crushed them.

"It's a bad eight miles to Christleton locks," he said. "Worse than ploughing a field to steer down here." And sure enough there was that occasional hesitancy when we touched the mud, or that heeling over on a bend to show that our bottom and the canal bed were on too close terms. How he would manage on the return, thirty inches deep in the water, seemed a problem. We fell to discussing the run, and he told me that his fastest round trip was to leave Oldbury at 3 a.m. on a Tuesday and be back there unloading by 4 p.m. on the Friday. We had a 19-mile journey before us now, and should reach Ellesmere Port before noon. For seven years, until just after the war, Les had been horse-drawn up here, taking a week on the return journey, and a horse-boat had continued on the run until only a few months earlier. It was now transferred to the Coventry – Banbury route on the Oxford cut.

A fine panorama of the Clwydian Hills had unfolded far to our left, while a mile or so ahead there rose a church tower to mark Rowton, on whose moor in 1645 Cromwell's stiffnecks defeated the Royalist forces. Rowton tower, one of the typical solid square edifices of Shropshire and Cheshire, loses its dignity from the silly little spirelet mounted on it. Several items of interest were telescoped into a few hundred yards at Christleton. First we passed one of the Llangollen Canal 'trench boats', built up high amidships into a shocking houseboat, surely the most uncongenial of all dwellings, where the residents must feel a constant urge to up anchor and follow the passing boats. Bridge 121 had a winding pool bordered by well-tended gardens and lawns, with flower-beds and rockery down to the canal edge. Then came, of all things, an aviary — cages of exotic tropical birds beneath some lordly beeches which laved their roots in the canal. Facing them, Ernest Butler's 'Christleton Mills' rose above the water and dispensed a pleasant mealy odour far and wide.

From the top lock of the 'Christleton Five' we had our first view of Chester, and at a cottage Annie bought a large bowl of apples from a woman who saves her illustrated magazines for the Berridge family — Les is the only one able to read. I took my morning consitutional down these locks — all the work necessary was to draw the paddles and open and close the gates, as the boats were breasted up and travelling under TOWY's power. A new feature of canal architecture was now occurring — a small round red brick toll house with beehive roof — and beside Greenfield lock a housing estate was being erected, source of much interest to Annie who has never lived in a house but thinks it might be better than the boats.

Chester was now fully displayed before us, the dominant features being a remarkable building like a very tall lighthouse or a somewhat plumper factory chimney with windows spiralling round it which rose from a lead works, the Shot Tower and the lofty bulk of a seed warehouse. Framed between them, and straight ahead along the canal, was the red stone cathedral. I have never been in Chester Cathedral, which is doubtless more attractive than the face it shows to the world. The exterior is as ugly as its name — St. Werburgh's — with a turreted tower in the worst tradition of prison architecture, and tawdry crocketed pinnacles. At any minute I expected a black flag to be hoisted on the flagpole.

The morning sun warm on our backs, we cruised into the heart of Roman Deva, with Canal Side on our left hand where houses look on the canal like a Dutch quayside, without even a railing between road and water. Here is a large corn merchant's, its loading bays bearing evidence of much canal traffic in the past, but a queue of red lorries of British Road Services showing where that trade had gone. There was a colour and tradition about our narrow boats that these hurtling usurpers will never give the world. I once did a journalistic journey by B.R.S. lorry from Birmingham to Glasgow, and lived in fear and trembling all the way. Give me my four miles an hour on the cut.

Slicing between the cathedral and the Gaumont Palace, the canal runs beneath the city walls and King Charles's Tower, where that unhappy monarch watched the return of his defeated troops from Rowton Moor. Northgate Bridge carried its traffic high above our deep trench. Only a few yards away Chester's 'Bridge of Sighs' spans the canal, its iron railings gone — sacrificed to war — and access to it now bricked up from the Bluecoat School on the one end, and some other building opposite. Emerging from this sheer cutting at the top of Nor'gate Locks we had a superb view across miles of Cheshire into Flintshire with its gracefully rolling Clwydian Hills, Moel Fammau prominent in the undulating chain. Half a mile ahead electric pylons bestrode the meadows, while above a field in the middle distance fluttered a snowstorm of gulls.

Tom Roberts, lock-keeper at Nor'gate these 41 years, whose father did the job before him, must be an adept at those puzzles where one is afflicted with unlikely numbers of black and white men to be ferried across a river without mixing the colours in the boat. Nor'gate Locks are treble chamber locks — four gates to three chambers — and they descend 60 feet in three falls of 20, 22, and 18 feet. Tom's problems in conserving water are those of raising some boats while lowering others, and he has had five boats in the locks simultaneously, some locking up, some down. From the bottom of the first treble locks, where we turned north on our last eight miles to Ellesmere Port, three more locks drop down another 60 feet to the river Dee, but are not much used.

The morning had become lovely, white clouds scudding before a lively breeze over a sky of rain-washed blue. Adding to my pleasure, a newspaper had come aboard at Chester containing the joyful news of the downfall of Mossadek. After all, he is indelibly associated in our minds with oil, and our errand was to collect diesel oil, so he is not entirely out of place here. If ever one man deliberately pursued a course which might have resulted in world war and millions of deaths, it was Mossadek. The morning was the brighter when I knew that justice still worked out sometimes. There was also news that England had won the 'Ashes', and that the whole nation had been 'cricket crazy' on the previous day. I thanked my stars that I had been dwelling in a world apart — and a sane world at that.

Mrs Berridge provided an enormous breakfast of bacon and egg from the little coal stove in KUBINA's cabin, and I ate mine on the roof, revelling in the sunshine. Annie, who had taken over the tiller on TOWY, was threatened loudly that her breakfast would be withheld if she did not keep the boats straight, as things were being upset in KUBINA's cabin. And certainly, both the girls' steering was haphazard, though how they managed to tack to and fro so much without going aground was a constant wonder to me. Good steering, a pride and joy with me and an essential of Les's stock-in-trade, was just a job to the girls. I found myself discussing education with Mrs Berridge. She regretted young Leslie's refusal to go back to school in Birmingham, and hoped the other boys would get some education so that they might find 'better' jobs. Making due allowance for the rose-coloured spectacles through which I view canal life, I think that view, praiseworthy though it be, is wrong. Education to enable them to read and write for their own entertainment, yes. But the degree of education likely in a secondary modern school, attended from a hostel, is not likely to raise a canal boy above the lowest stratum of the working class. If, at best, it makes him a machine-minder, his wages will be no better than those of a boatman — £13 with certain additions on this round trip of less than a week, without any outgoings on rent or rates.

But as a boatman he is regarded by all classes of society, not as inhabiting one of the lowest social grades, but as a race apart, guardians — maybe unwittingly — of a tradition; as something so much more interesting and exciting than a factory worker. Hours are long, work is hard in patches, with long idyllic spells in good weather and the harvest of the hedgerows there for the picking. There is no foreman at the boatman's back, no immediate supervision. His measure of freedom is greater than that of the house-bound worker. Conditions are crowded, sanitary facilities primitive. But given the choice between working in factory or office without chances of considerable promotion, and being a boatman, I would choose the latter.

Thus philosophising, we came up to the brown tower of Stoke church among its trees, our last bit of country. Already dozens of silver oil tanks stretched before us along the line of the Mersey, with flambeaux where the waste is burned raised torch-like above. To eastward prominent headlands faced out across the tidal sands of the river — Helsby Hill above the marshes, and Weston Point, where the Weaver Navigation enters the Manchester Ship Canal, overhanging Runcorn. Back inland stretched the uplands of Delamere Forest, back to Beeston whence we had come that morning, and the line of the Peckforton Hills. Two miles out of Ellesmere Port we passed Clayton's SPEY with its butty OHIO on the 'long snubber' as the towrope is called. And in a galvanised sheeting warehouse basin, Les pointed out a broad-beamed barge, a 'flat' as they are called in these parts. The broader the beam the nearer the sea, and we were soon in the Shropshire Union's quarter million pound dock area of Ellesmere Port.

Down the three locks we went, and out on to the wide waterway of Manchester Ship Canal, divided by only a narrow sea wall from the Mersey. In the past, Clayton boats sometimes waited as long as two days for a tug to take them the mile and a half to Stanlow where they ship their oil. So Mr Clayton took out a licence for his own steerers to navigate the ship Canal, and they get an additional 15 shillings for the feat. We travelled breasted-up past large ocean-going vessels, and came alongside FORTH and RIBBLE at the oil installations. The narrow boats, which usually fill their own native canals, were quite lost, and barely noticeable in the much grander scale of this important waterway.

It took only half-an-hour to fill our holds, 45 tons divided almost equally between the two boats, and the hatches were clamped down on the treacly oil. Then Les let me take the tiller to get the feel of steering breasted up. This was perfectly easy even though the canal was so wide that there was no fear of grounding. With tugs and coasters passing us from seaward, their bow waves would send up a waterspout, shooting along the slight gap between our pair of boats, but we rode quite steadily. Mrs Berridge was, however, obviously ill at ease in these spacious waters, and kept an even sharper eye than usual on the children and on shipping approaching or coming up astern. But, slowing down while a tug went by, I turned our joint noses for the locks, and we came safely off the Ship Canal.

We had travelled some 90 miles from Oldbury at about four m.p.h. While I was being driven madly back to Birmingham at 60 m.p.h., our car crossed Prees Heath airfield where a maniac in a Meteor dived at us at 600 m.p.h. Every day fools — and worse — crash in these hellish jets to the infinite danger of lives and property below. Let us keep our narrow boats so that in an age gone mad on speed, men may look at them and marvel at their four miles an hour.

CHAPTER SEVEN

By narrow boat, car, tug, and Shanks's Pony I
explore the waterways between Birmingham and
Hull, sample the night life of Nottingham's
waterside, and grind over the shoals of Humber
to a final mooring at Hull.

I take my pleasures the hard way. Instead of rising at 4.30 a.m. I
could have had two more hours in bed and boarded TAUNTON and
BEGONIA at Salford Bridge with darker Birmingham, the six Camp
Hill Locks, and the Saltley five already done. Instead I was at
Sampson Road Wharf by 6 a.m. as we cast off and sent ripples
forward to shatter the eastern pinnacles of Holy Trinity Church,
faithfully reflected in the still water of a grey September morning.
But buoying me up and overcoming the privations of early rising
and bow-hauling, was the thought that here was beginning the
last of my four half-cardinal journeys to the sea, the north-eastern
leg to the Humber and Hull. This had been the most difficult to
arrange for there is no through traffic. But the South-Eastern
Division of British Waterways had fixed my lift to Fazeley, while
North-Eastern Division were seeing me through from
Nottingham to Hull. I had to cover nearly 50 miles in between on
my own, and in good enough time to make my connection at
Nottingham.

This was the first time I had travelled in open boats — TOWY
and others were flush-decked, and NORMAN CHAMBERLAIN is, of
course, built up. TAUNTON's blue and yellow of British
Waterways clashed with the traditional red, green, and yellow of
the butty BEGONIA, which still bore the proud name of Fellows,
Morton & Clayton though one of a British Waterways pair. It
was a Saturday morning, and just a week earlier the boats had left
Brentford with a cargo of aluminium ingots for Birmingham.
Now they were ordered empty to Glascote, near Tamworth, to

165

pick up coal for one of the mills on the Grand Union in the
Watford area, and I was accompanying them as far as Fazeley.

Skipper Peter Tyler, a cheery little chap of 37, whose arms
swung violently sideways in nautical fashion as he hurried to open
the locks, had been born on the cut at Marsworth bottom lock —
'agin the public'. His Dad, a hearty 74, crowned with a pork-pie
hat and sporting a medalled watch-chain across his waistcoat, who
was at TAUNTON's tiller while Peter and I bow-hauled BEGONIA,
first saw the light of day in a boat cabin at Calcutt Locks, near
Leamington. What volumes of protesting cries must have been
heard by many a canal lock! 'Mother', a comfortable figure who
fitted felicitously into the cabin doorway, told me she had "reared
12 of 'em with Fellows, Morton". The remainder of our
complement were Mrs Tyler, Junior, and baby Linda, 14 months
old. Struck by the repetition of the Berridge baby's name I asked
if Linda was a favourite canal name, but learned that it had been

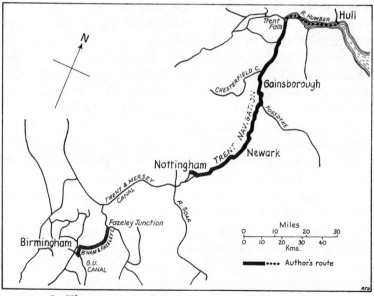

9: The waterways between Birmingham and Hull

given to the youngest Tyler by nurses in the post-natal hospital. Mr Tyler, Senior, and 'Mother' were only recently back on the boats after a spell of retirement ashore at Smethwick.

No amount of infatuation with canals can render this 'bottom road' to Salford Bridge anything but filthy, environed as it is with engine sheds and sidings, with odorous gasworks, with arch after purplish arch carrying Birmingham's traffic, and with locks whose sides are thick and ebony-hued with oil. But beauty blossoms even here when oil-bursts erupt on the murky surface of the canal into kaleidoscopic changes of colour: deep glowing red, purple, violet, emerald, silver — ever-widening circles until a lock below is opened and the circles become first a broken mosaic pavement, and then rainbow streaks as the water gathers momentum towards the sluices. We greeted a railway guard leaning from his van as it rumbled across a bridge where the beat of our engine rose in a crescendo, a workman cycling along the towpath, a factory stoker whose boilers opened on the canal, and two window-cleaners busy with their leathers so that men at the bench may the better enjoy the passing pageant of canal life.

In the pound between Camp Hill and Saltley locks I steered, reciting the while to Peter the names of boats lying at a depot, to be told in return how, despite being unable to read, he once did a rail journey from Coventry to London without getting lost, and even coped with "them tube things they 'as in London". He would ask how many stations there were to his destination, and then count the stops.

There is a stop-lock at the toll office of the old Birmingham & Warwick Junction Navigation, opposite the power station where British Electricity Authority boats are frequent, and clearing this we crossed the River Tame and poled round a sharp right hand bend into the Birmingham & Fazeley Canal at Salford Bridge beside old hulks full of green slime and burr marigold. This Fazeley cut is essentially an artery for coal. The usual round trip for Grand Union boats begins from London to Birmingham with a variety of goods — rubber, copper or aluminium ingots, plates of zinc, milk powder from New Zealand, dates and concentrated Italian tomatoes for a sauce factory, Sicily almonds in sacks, tinned salmon. These are discharged at Tyseley or Sampson Road wharfs, with timber at Cartwrights, Olton, and the boats continue empty by way of Fazeley to the Coventry Canal which serves the Warwickshire coalfield. Loaded with coal for mills near London the boats remain on the Coventry Canal to rejoin the Grand Union at Braunston.

Inward bound to Birmingham two Element horse-boats laden with coal passed us. "Hold out Mother," shouted Dad from TAUNTON to his wife at BEGONIA's tiller as IRIS came alongside. Motors defer to horse-drawn craft, and knowing that there was another Element boat coming, Peter hooted at each blind bridge to avoid any collision, which would have impeded the other rather than us.

There is an interesting tunnel at Birlec where the factory is built out over several hundred yards of canal and supported on concrete pillars beyond the towpath, which gives an arcaded effect to the waterway. Around the Bromford Bridges the Dunlop factories loom like two liners across their playing fields where, at the canalside, an unusual weather-vane is raised above the pavilion — a batsman about to drive, whose uplifted bat points into the wind. On we went, by a paint factory which was spilling much of its sepia product into the water and much of its odour into the air, and past Tyburn House pub — or 'public' in canal parlance — a mock medieval manor house in yellow stone. Chipmunk training planes hopped up and down like fleas on Castle Bromwich aerodrome. Much of the countryside into which we were moving was built on Birmingham's sewage, and there was the not unpleasing smell of effluent in the atmosphere as we passed the Minworth Works of the Tame and Rea District Drainage Board, where sprinklers spread fairy-fountains of spray like a low mist between the long lines of poplars which usually mark such places.

The bridges on these pounds all have recesses where stop planks are kept, and all have their nameplates. What local history must repose in them! Brace Factory Bridge is self-explanatory; Trout Pool Bridge in an industrial area is less easily explained; and proceeding countrywards, Hanson's at the city boundary, Cater's low with many scrape marks, Wigginshall Road with a silver and green converted butty CAMBRIAN, Broad Balk, Curdworth Church Bridge at our first cutting, Fox's, Wilday's Farm, Marston Field, and Cheatle's Farm Bridge at 'The Dog & Jacket' which opens a hospitable door on the cut adjacent to a farmyard. Among the bridges was Plum Pudding Tunnel, exactly the length of our pair of boats, and so confined that the chimneys had to be lowered hurriedly.

Just before Baylis's Bridge, Mr Tyler, Senior, pointed to trees fringing the canal on our left to say that there was once a gunpowder store among them. This prompted the further reminiscence that his old Dad left TILBURY a fortnight before she was blown up in the Regent's Park disaster, the classical canal calamity in 1874 when several boatmen were killed as boats laden with explosives went sky high.

Disentangled of Birmingham and its tentacles we dropped down the three Minworth Locks and there was open country on either hand, with many large fields of cabbages. Martins were swooping along the canal with wide open mouths drinking in flight. Some distance ahead we could see the spoil mounds of the first of the collieries. Behind us the canal was a shining silver trail in the sun for the afternoon had turned out delightful. At Curdworth top lock young Mrs Tyler bought some 'taters' from a cottage, and the huge cooling towers of Hams Hall power station were abeam on our right. The 'Curdworth eleven' are fairly wide apart and though we bow-hauled in some short pounds at the longer ones TAUNTON gave BEGONIA a 'snatch' — the word referring to the actual moment when the short coupling rope from the motor takes the first strain in towing the butty. There is not much canal stabling still used, though ancient stables are always features of canal architecture. But there was ample evidence at the back of The Old Bakery and Grocery Stores, Curdworth, that the 'good stabling' is still used, obviously by Element's horses. Beside Curdworth No 10 stood an old night-watchman's hut, a tiny circular red brick structure crowned by a witch's hat minus the brim, but with a chimney protruding at the side — a place of lonely night vigil in use up to 20 years ago. At the bottom lock a house bore the Roman figures for 1820, and a disused wooden swivel bridge showed one way of moving cattle across the canal in bygone days. One of the early objections to canals, in addition to their splitting in two farms and estates, was that they would prove impediments to fox hunting — more power to the cut.

The River Tame was now close on our right. Some half mile beyond it a quarry had made a red rift on a hillside at Bosthill, and my old O.S. map showed an aerial ropeway from it to the canal. 'Mother', with whom I was enjoying a cup of tea at BEGONIA's tiller, recalled when boats used to load from that ropeway, though a tangle of hemp agrimony almost covered any relic of this. A second swivel bridge still operates before Fazeley alongside a striking ornamental bridge for pedestrians on Drayton Manor Estate. Two towers, like the bases of factory chimneys, with spiral steps inside them, are connected over the canal by a wooden footbridge with a handrail and wire netting for safety.

We were now in Fazeley where the tape mills were working full time, though there cannot be much call for their once staple product, stay laces. At the junction at 2.30 p.m. I left the Tylers who, having brought me 15 miles, were turning right into the Coventry Canal, while I was travelling left 11 miles to Fradley. The Birmingham & Fazeley Canal was constructed in the eighth decade of the 18th Century after the Birmingham Canal had proved so successful. The Coventry Canal, then under construction, had come to a standstill at Fazeley in 1782, 11 miles short of the southernmost point of the Trent & Mersey Canal at Fradley. So in that year the proprietors of the Trent & Mersey agreed to complete the 11 miles from Fazeley to Fradley, and to convey part of the length to the Coventry Canal proprietors at cost. It was ultimately opened for traffic in July 1790, and the northern 5½ miles between Fradley Junction and Whittington Brook were acquired by the Coventry Canal Company while the southern half remained part of the Birmingham & Fazeley. Thus arises the anomaly of the old Coventry Canal finishing at Fazeley, and recommencing 5½ miles northward for a final section of 5½ miles to the Trent & Mersey Canal.

The Tylers predicted much woe at my embarking on so long a walk, and, truth to tell, I had my own misgivings. The distance was negligible, but I had bruised my right heel while jumping from TAUNTON — how badly I could not yet tell — and I wondered if it would cope with the walk. I removed shoe and sock to find a large bruise beneath my ankle. When I began walking, my heel was tender but the walk seemed possible, though having now seen the canal I felt doubtful of any lift. So, shouldering my pack, I headed north. For 15 minutes the friendly chug of TAUNTON was borne to my ears on the still air. Then it died, and the link was broken. I was on my own. The towpath was neglected and had an awkward camber which, aided by a hawthorn hedge with berries, almost shoved me in the cut, an attractive waterway, cool, reedy, and crystal clear among its many aquatic plants. Occasionally, at a much-appreciated gap in the venomous hedge, I caught a glimpse eastward of Tamworth. Modern ramparts of red brick villas guarded this ancient capital of Mercia with its castle and the massive church which dominates the town, frowning contemptuously on an impudent stripling of a white tower to its left.

I was approaching the village of Hopwas which nestles on the canal and the Tame beneath the conifer-spiked ridge of Hays Wood. From the acreage of glass it would seem to have a thriving nursery trade. At Hopwas I knew I should find the first telephone of my walk, and I had to ring Mr Webb, a British Waterways official at Nottingham, to find out if the tug on which I was to travel to Hull would leave Nottingham on the morrow or Monday. To my regret it was Sunday; so I had to alter my plans and accelerate my pace, for it was suggested I sleep aboard that night. My original intention had been to join the Trent & Mersey at Fradley Junction and stay the night in Alrewas, leaving some 20 miles of the canal and about 10 of the River Trent to cover on Sunday and Monday morning, reaching Nottingham in time to catch the tug at noon on Monday. Now a glance at my map suggested that the best plan might be to leave the Coventry Canal a couple of miles short of Fradley on Rykneld Street, bus into Burton, and entrain to Nottingham.

Back on the canal bank how I regretted the need for this speed. My way lay along the loveliest length of canal I had yet seen anywhere, lightly tree-fringed but with sunshine dappling through to a more comfortable grassy towpath which added heather and harebells to the usual flora, and lighting the limpid depths where fish rose lazily through waving weed to ring the surface. Below, to the right, the Tame pursued its unexciting way through fields to the Trent, much less attractive than my canal. The afternoon was warm and utterly tranquil, with long gentle rolls of autumnal cloud from which no harm could come. Coloured butterflies flirted everywhere with the September flowers, and the leaves had that touch of advancing age which gives them character. There was just enough breeze to set each leaf rustling separately on the poplars without moving the branches, so that the trees stirred gently and sighed for departing summer. The afternoon wrapped me in the generous embrace of a mature and opulent woman, so much better than the alternate hot and cold vacillations of that coy wanton, Spring. I would have lingered and savoured those embraces, given myself up to dalliance with them, but I had to hurry. At Hopwas a woman in a pretty flower garden had told me that a pleasure boat was travelling north half an hour ahead of me. Its track through the weeds yawned tantalisingly open yet, and I hoped to overtake it round any bend. But it was not to be. I was spurred on, too, by the hope that some traffic might join the canal at Huddlesford, the junction with the Wyrley & Essington. So I pressed on harder, seeming to spurn the beauty of my surroundings, and the canal now running parallel with the main L.M.S. line, my urge for speed was mocked by hurtling expresses — the London – Glasgow and the London – Manchester.

To my left I had a view of the famous Ladies of the Vale, the three spires of Lichfield Cathedral. Then, like snipers from the tall bracken across the canal, came the staccato crackle of rifle-firing at Whittington Barracks, grossest insult to the loveliness and peace of the afternoon. It was 5.40 p.m. when I reached Huddlesford, and one glance down the straight reed-narrowed expanse of the Wyrley and Essington, stretching westward to Brownhills and Walsall, convinced me that the junction in no way enhanced my chances of a lift. The inevitable junction 'public' was 'The

Plough' and the canal was guarded by a pair of swans and seven cygnets, while a flotilla of ivory ducks cruised nearby.

One mile more and I left the canal where first it approached Rykneld Street, just north of Streethay, and was soon on a bus for Burton-on-Trent. For four miles from Alrewas the Trent & Mersey Canal ran alongside the road, worse maintained than the canal I had been walking, a condition suggesting that my hopes of a lift on working or pleasure boats along that length had been ill-founded. But at Barton-under-Needwood, where it veered away from the road, there were signs that it had been cleared. I was glad of the rest in the bus for I had become footsore from walking awkwardly to protect my bruised heel. Now, I felt, my exertions were over. Had I but known!

It was nine o'clock when the train pulled in to Nottingham Midland. My instructions were to go to Trent Lane where the tug TEES was lying at British Waterways Wharf. A railwayman in my compartment had provided precise directions for reaching the wharf, warning me that it was a half-hour walk. I prefer making my own way to peering anxiously for an unknown stop from a bus, and I had no difficulty here — Arkwright Street, Kirk White Street East, over a bridge, through a poor neighbourhood which reminded me of Belfast south of the Lagan. Then I skirted Notts County football ground, caught a glimpse of a milk factory — and walked into 'the smell'. I have grovelled in Birmingham sewers, written up the sewage disposal works, and that section of the Salvage Department which renders down bad meat for various purposes. I have smelt hide factories, meat markets, fish quays and the like, but never have I suffered a stink so powerful, so all-pervading, as 'the smell' of Nottingham. The night was quite still, yet it took me 10 minutes, all in a residential area, to gasp my way through it.

Panting, I emerged, only to be assailed by a lesser effluvium, this time of a chemical or engineering nature. Bearing up manfully I turned into Trent Lane, dark and remote despite a greyhound race meeting over some tall boards. The land came to a dead end with mention of a ferry and some steps descending into an abyss. I found a door in a locked gateway, stepped through it, and was on a wharf, deserted and dismal in the darkness. Gabled warehouses loomed above the river, which snaked oily and forbidding below. The shapes of several boats broke that repulsive current, so I bellowed "TEES" several times. Getting no reply, I groped warily along the quayside like someone in a gangster film, until, guiltily rounding the angle of a building, I bumped, to our mutual consternation, into a youth who said that TEES was at Meadow Lane near the milk factory.

What was another mile to my ill-used feet? I retraced my steps, past the greyhound track, through the minor smell, into 'the smell' and out of it, and beside the milk factory I found a notice 'British Waterways' with an arrow pointing into a pitch-black canyon between two buildings. I wandered cautiously through this gloom to come out again on the riverside just downstream of Trent Bridge. The only sign of life was in an upstairs window of what might have been a lock-keeper's house, for access to it was possible only across lock gates astride a canal. Gingerly I essayed the crossing, but my assault on an office door brought no reply. Apart from a fleet of ghostly cabin cruisers across the river, the only boat in sight was lying in the shadow of the quayside beneath a factory, but my efforts to reach it were baulked by the sudden complete cessation of the river wall.

Again I raised my voice — "TEES ahoy, TEES, TEES," and did not desist until a mocking reply wafted across the river, 'Suppers'. Time was getting on. There were several reasons for finding TEES. I might be expected, though this seemed unlikely in the continued absence of a reception committee; I was too grubby to go to a good hotel, and the chances of a boarding house being open were receding every minute. Besides, I was on my mettle, tired though I was. I wanted to find that confounded tug. The next move was to phone the home of my contact, Mr Webb, but on my way to a call-box I made a detour in tentative search of accommodation — up Kirk White Street, down Arkwright Street. Then I scanned the riverside from Trent Bridge hoping to see TEES, only to disturb a number of Nottingham's notoriously beautiful girls in the arms of young men on the dark benches conveniently situated for the purpose.

Mr Webb, when I phoned, was having his own troubles, being out on a lock replacement job at Torksey, where Foss Dyke enters the Trent. But Mrs Webb phoned one or two alternative places in search of TEES and rang me back at my call-box. This brought us to 11 p.m. and I learned that TEES was definitely at Meadow Lane, probably the boat I could see downstream, and that it was accessible through some vegetation. It was, I thought, too late to wake the crew, so I returned to two 'Bed & Breakfasts', to find each of them besieged by fellows from Newark who had missed the last bus — alas the fatal beauty of these Nottingham girls! Neither had accommodation, so I plunged once more into the canyon toward the river and surveyed the undergrowth. There was now a light downstairs in the lock-house, so finding my way to the backdoor regardless of any dog, I knocked, in hope of a torch or a guide. A startled female voice cried "Who's there?", and to my query if the boat downstream was TEES replied in the affirmative, adding that it was quite get-at-able — via the undergrowth. So, negotiating the lock for the fourth time in the darkness, I shoved gingerly through the willow-herb and mugwort, winning my way unscathed to the concrete quay beside the factory. The boat was a frightful distance below me. I shouted, but went unheeded. Carefully in the Stygian gloom I sought the usual iron steps, found them, and fearfully lowered myself towards the scarce-seen river.

The deck was of steel plates, and my tread should have awakened the dead. I inspected a lifebelt. Yes, this was TEES, but apparently deserted. I tried everything vaguely resembling a hatch but could budge nothing. The wheelhouse seemed to be locked. There was only one thing for it — to doss in the dinghy. I tried it. It might be bearable at the moment, but in two hours time — what? So I ate an orange, slung on my pack once more, mounted that vertical ladder, breasted the undergrowth again, and went in final search of a bed. A factory watchman gave me a cup of water and directions to the police station, for I contemplated throwing myself on the mercies of the Force. Off I went again, up Kirk White Street to Arkwright Street. It was midnight. I was very tired. My mind began making play on those street names in repeated refrain: 'Arkwright, Kirk White; spinning frames and spinning rhymes; Arkwirght, Kirk White; spinning. . . . ' I could have searched my memory of any other English poet for a quotation apt to my circumstances, but of the obscure Kirk White I knew not a line.

At the police station a constable was most optimistic, not being faced with my problem. I need only knock at the Bowden Hotel in Queen's Drive, which in desperation I did. A dog barked, a light was lit, bolts withdrawn, and an elderly man in singlet and pyjama trousers appeared at the half-open door. I stated my requirements. I was a scruffy sight in polo-neck sweater, and carrying a pack I swore never again to blanco when I knocked it off from the army. So I asked the charge, was told 15 shillings, and proffered a £1 note. Relief shone in the pyjamad one's eyes. He had a single room. "Would I like a wash?" I would — 'the benison of hot water'. A middling soft bed. 'Arkwright, Kirk White, spinning frames. . .' Sleep.

Life looked much brighter next morning when I made my way in Sabbath sunshine to Trent Bridge. There I leaned contentedly on the parapet and gazed upstream, feeling that Nottingham had made exceptional good use of its river as a pleasure resort, what with grass, trees, and concrete steps for the many fishermen. Idly I crossed the road and glanced downstream to see what TEES was like by daylight. And I nearly jumped into the river. Her mooring was vacant. Birmingham's water links with the sea! This, it seemed, was the missing link! I rushed round to the lock-house and introduced myself to the lock-keeper's wife as her nocturnal visitor. She knew of me from a phone call that morning from Mr Webb. TEES had moved down to Trent Lane to fuel, but would be back for me at noon. Meanwhile, how about a cup of tea?

Over this I learned that the canal I had crossed so precariously four times during the night was the Nottingham Canal which ran back through the lace city, and after achieving a junction with the Beeston cut, struck north, west, and north again to skirt Ilkeston and link various collieries with the Trent. Its busy days were over, and only an occasional British Waterways lighter or pleasure boat uses it. The river, however, teemed with activity — rowing boats, pleasure cruises to Colwick Park, single scullers, fours, and eights, their boathouse behind the line of artificial miniature sand dunes which separated Nottingham Forest's ground from the Trent on the far bank.

At noon, at long last, I boarded TEES and met her crew. Bill Johnson, the skipper, was a Nottingham man; Jack (Nobby) Clark, the engineer, was from Hull; and the mate, Bob Hodgson, had recently returned from National Service in Hong Kong, where the Army achieved the unusual feat of putting a square peg in a square hole by assigning Bob to the Royal Army Service Corps (Water Transport Section). TEES is a motor vessel, a tug, built at Warren's Shipyard, New Holland; her length 82 feet, beam 14½ feet, capable of 10 knots solo, but content with 5½ to 6 when towing. She has a mast to carry her riding light which is surmounted by another white light to indicate that she has a tow. This usually consists of 'dumb barges', while TEES has cargo space for 40 tons herself. I was shown TEES' birth certificate — her Certificate of Registration as a Canal Boat. Registered under the Canal Boats Act, 1877, her registration authorities are the Lord Mayor, aldermen, and citizens of Nottingham, and the place to which she is registered for purposes of the Education Act, should children live aboard, is also Nottingham. The Certificate was dated August 16th, 1932.

TEES' normal run is from Hull to Nottingham with barges carrying a variety of merchanidise — grain, timber, spelter, boxwood, concentrated tomatoes — imports discharged into the tug and her barges direct from sea-going ships. British Waterways have warehouses at Nottingham where these commodities are stored to be distributed by road; boxwood, newsprint, and spelter being some of the items which find their way to Birmingham. If necessary TEES goes to Goole, Grimsby, Leeds by the Aire & Calder Navigation, or York by the Ouse Navigation. Her run from Hull to Newark is 73½ miles, 68 of them to Cromwell Lock being tidal. This can be done in 8 hours, or it may take 16, for TEES has an implacable enemy, the river bed, and groundings cause many delays. Consequently she has water ballast tanks fore and aft, and these were being filled at Meadow Lane. Her last trip from

Hull had started at 3 p.m. on Friday, towing one barge with flour for Nottingham Co-op; one with bales of paper; and one with barley for Newark. Travelling without a stop, the convoy had reached Nottingham — minus the Newark barge — in 22 hours, at 1 p.m. on Saturday.

With a black cloud of smoke from the funnel just aft of the 'wheel-box' (never 'wheel-house') we were off, towing TRENT NO. 35, on a fine stream, past the racecourse and between meadows lined with fishermen. Astern, the prominent features of Nottingham rose clear against a blue sky: the castle, the Council House dome, and an old windmill, taken over as a boot polish factory. In two miles we passed through Colwick flood lock into Holme Cut, an artificial half-mile which circumvents the river's long meander northward. At the next lock, where we passed back to the river, there was considerable activity afoot, for a sluice weir was being constructed, the better to control the river level, and I went ashore and looked down into the deep bed for the reservoir, 150 yards square. There is a corresponding spoil mound across the river at the tail of Holme Lock, and this will no doubt be used to fill in the meander, for the intention is to direct the whole flow of the Trent through Holme Cut. This alteration will see the end of Colwick flood lock, and bigger boats will be able to reach Nottingham.

Off the British Sugar Corporation factory we took up another tow, TRENT NO 37, and continued downstream with the two dumb barges breasted up astern, their bluff bows jutting either side of TEES. The banks were now meadows cut away sharply into sheer red clifflets with a drop of about 8 feet. At Radcliffe-on-Trent a line of tree-clad red hills turned the river sharply northward, the bend being a lively resort of caravans, shacks, cabin cruisers and yachts. Trent has its own bore, the 'eagre', which is felt as far inland as Cromwell Lock. We were creating our own eagre, and it sent two children scampering off a little beach at Radcliffe, leaving their sand-castles to be washed away. All afternoon the waves in our wake caused fishermen to skip from exposed islands of grass or muddy promontories, dragging clothing, keep-nets, bait tins, and food baskets above the wash.

Our crew were thoughtful about this and always shouted a warning or slowed down if children were bathing and likely to be endangered. Most Trent fishermen seemed aware of this hazard to their sport, but when the rare exception was deep in contemplation we generally managed to appraise him of the inconvenience in time.

Nobby brought me TEES' log-book, and I noted some 'causes of delay'. 'towing from Cromwell to Nether Lock in dense fog'. 'Running half speed, No 33 rope broke.' 'Only two hours tide from Hull, under ebb from Owston ferry.' 'Under ebb from Gainsborough.' 'Delayed at Dunham one hour, boat grounded.' Grounding was fairly frequent, and I was able to appreciate on the morrow just what an obstacle it is.

Near the ferry at Stoke Bardolph there was an outflow of effluent from the sewage works, and whatever may be thought about river pollution the fish would seem to revel in it if the con- centration of fishermen immediately downstream of the conduit was any criterion. A line of Lombardy poplars appearing astern, Nobby asked me which two trees were farthest apart, and I regret that I gave the problem a lengthy study before realising that the answer was those at each end of the row. As we approached the three graceful spans of Gunthorpe Bridge, the skipper blew loud and long on our hooter for no apparent purpose. This was, however, to warn Gunthorpe Lock of our approach and, it also warning a goodly crowd, our locking was done to a large gallery. What with the crews of our barges and our own crew, the sluice handles were soon manned, four to each pair of gates, like the wheels of a mangle. Another wheel on either side of the lock wall opened the gates on a rack and pinion system. The river runs round each of these locks over a weir, and it was at Gunthorpe recently that a barge went on the weir in a 'fresh' to be towed off by TEES after the crew had spent a night on their precarious perch. We locked down into a veritable ice-floe of detergent bergs churned up by the weir, and as I looked back the thigh-booted anglers at the foot of the weir were waist deep in soapsuds.

'The smug and silver Trent'. With the turbulence of Gunthorpe weir left behind, the river was absolutely unrippled, reflecting clouds, banks, and trees as in a mirror. Surely Shakespeare must have seen Trent to have coined that perfect description, in which I never interpret 'smug' as a derogatory term. How many who know the expression know its origin? In 1403 the Earl of March, Owen Glendower, and Hotspur, rose against Henry IV. In anticipation of success they divided the Kingdom between them, Trent to be the boundary between their domains. Five miles upstream of Gainsborough the river made two large ox-bows westward. Ultimately the Trent would shift its course, cutting across the neck of these loops thus transferring some of Hotspur's land to March, hence Hotspur, in *Henry IV, Part I,* Act 3, Scene I:

'I'll have the current in this place damm'd up;
And here the smug and silver Trent shall run
In a new channel, fair and evenly.'

Hotspur need not have worried. It was not until 1792 and 1797 that the decapitation of the loops occurred, and a further 100 years elapsed before the land thus left west of Trent was consigned by Lincolnshire to Nottinghamshire to preserve the river as the county boundary.

As we approached Hazelford Lock, a lilliputian range of wooded hills accompanied us on our right, usually one field back from the river but at times falling directly into it. At Hoveringham a squat grey church and a few red houses peeped over a shoulder of these gentle hills at the Elm Tree Inn across the river, and here I was taken down into the hot and quaking engine-room to be shown things that mean nothing to me. For the record, however, TEES is powered by a 160 h.p. Petters Automatic engine made at Yeovil, which will tow eight barges each carrying 100 tons, and it maintains the same speed with eight as with half the number. Nobby interested me more than his engine.

He had an excellent knowledge of the Trent, and a good repertoire of poetry with which he quoted our way downstream from the 'clear and cool' upper reaches of Kingsley's *River's Song* to Masefield's 'dirty British coaster' in the estuary. With 13 years service in the old Trent Navigation Company and British

Waterways he had been skipper of STOUR, engaged mainly in carrying gravel between Nottingham or Newark and Carlton or Collingham. Nobby subscribes to the general opinion that waterways maintenance is better since nationalisation, but feels that the new regime would be a little more human if it maintained some of the personal touches of the old company. These are mainly concerned with minor bonuses — for sculling a boat, for splicing big ropes and wires, for being able to swim (10 shillings a year) or to life-save (15 shillings a year). Nobby's STOUR once did Hull to Nottingham in 17½ hours.

Hazelford differs from other Trent locks in that the weir is on the left going downstream, and the lock-house is on an island, one of four or five that remain out of 13 between Shardlow, south of Nottingham, and the Humber 100 years ago, others being at Barton, Rampton, Normanton, and Torksey. Also at Hazelford is 'The Star & Garter'. Trent riverside inns are more like roadhouses than the small pubs on the Severn.

There had been a busy traffic in pleasure cruisers all afternoon, but at Hazelford we encountered British Waterways tug BARLOCK, which had left Hull at 2 p.m. on the previous day. One of its barges contained slab cattle cake from Egypt, the other the inevitable Italian tomatoes. Following close behind was a Medway Oil Storage Company's tanker with petroleum from Saltend, the Humber equivalent as a petroleum store of Severn's Avonmouth. But there was oil nearer than Saltend, for this whole countryside had been extensively bored of recent years and Eakring, not far distant on the southern fringe of the Dukeries, has the only oilfield of any pretensions in England, where over 10 million gallons were produced between 1939 and 1949.

The river was now swinging about like a Brindley canal, and the three chimneys of Staythorpe Power Station appeared in various directions from us. There were greetings from Charlie, the ferryman at Farndon, as we passed. His rowing boat was the least exotic craft in this popular resort of the gregarious human on pleasure bent. The afternoon was now overcast but delightfully warm and windless, and the seven yachts rounding the power station in a race were hard put to find even a zephyr for their white

wings. Those to whom everything manmade is a blot on the fair
face of nature are often particularly hard on power stations. Yet I
found Staythorpe most attractive, stretched for some hundred
yards along the left bank, until my eyes were drawn to Newark
spire across fields to the right. Soaring to 252 feet, it is 50 feet
longer than the church, St. Mary Magdalen. Thirteenth and
fourteenth centuries merge in this heavenward vision, not only
superbly beautiful in its own right, but gaining much more in
rising above a flat town unchallenged by any other building.

The Trent falls away over Amersham's long weir to veer
westward of Newark, and we entered the town along an artificial
cut. Several groups of anglers were clustered round the scales at
which their catches were being weighed. One, his rods packed
ready for the homeward way, bent to swill his face in the canal,
but as his cupped hands were lowered, so our suction withdrew
the water, He made a futile cast, to look up in astonishment and
jump clear of the returning inundation of our wash. Sunning
himself in the garden of a waterside home he has built since his
retirement, was an old engineer of the Trent Navigation
Company. Nobby waved a greeting, and told me that this man
used to tighten a nut with his fingers so that a spanner was
required to loosen it. Past several red brick maltings, and along an
old tower windmill without sails; past the junction of the River
Devon (long 'e') and we unhooked our tow at British Waterways
warehouse, to slide slowly to a mooring at Newark Basin, 300
yards upstream of the ruined wall of the castle where King John
died in 1216. A much-maligned character, a 'bad king' of the
schoolroom, John nevertheless held the fort while his feckless
brother Richard wasted the country's substance on his imbecile
foreign wars. Such, however, is the popular appeal of a fighting
man that the undeserving Lionheart is hero to John's villain.

The barges carried on downstream of their own momentum,
through the lock, to await us in the morning, and our skipper
hurried off the catch a train to his Nottingham home for the night.
Nobby and I sat on deck enjoying the peace of the late summer
evening. Nearby rose a tall Trent Navigation Company warehouse with an ancient wheel crane before it. A mealy smell came

from a red mill with a white dusting of flour at windows and ventilators. Fish rings spread on the canal disturbing the perfect upended reflections. This was contentment.

The distant view of Newark had impressed me most favourably, so that I should have been prepared for the closer impact when I entered it, quaintly, across a lock and up a narrow alley which brought me to the junction of Mill Gate and Castle Gate. Turning along the latter I was soon staring above the traffic at the facade of the Corn Exchange, now a ballroom. Built in 1847, an essay in Victorian baroque, it is surmounted by a nude Neptune or Father Time wrestling with an upturned cornucopia, and an equally naked though younger male, who seemed about to strike a dog clutched in his left hand with a wheatsheaf brandished in his right. A few steps further, and I was looking across a lawn where trees were assuming the golden tint of autumn, through the vacant arches and windows of the castle, at the quiet evening sky. 'The Royal Oak', a tiny pub opposite the castle grounds, has an attractive sign of Charles II performing his famous Boscobel act, and a gateway giving glimpses of a creeper-festooned courtyard.

I turned from Castle Gate into Kirk Gate, a street closed at its far end, or rather transported heavenward by that glorious steeple. Nothing about St. Mary's could possibly equal the spire, so I did not worry about its interior, continuing instead into the wide market square to discover a new enthusiasm. What a delight! What history overlooks those cobbles; the red and brown facade of the fourteenth century 'White Hart' in one corner with its long gallery window; 'The Saracen's Head' in the south centre where Jeannie Deans rested on her journey to London in Scott's *Heart of Midlothian*; the black and white half-timbered house with fluted red tiles where Prince Rupert stayed after his quarrel with Charles I on October 19th, 1645. In the south-west corner near the stately Town Hall once stood the house of Alderman Hercules Clay, destroyed on March 11th, 1643, during the second siege of loyal Newark, by a bombard aimed by the Cromwellians at the Governor's residence.

I found my greatest satisfaction in the hidden north-west corner. Squeezed between a Georgian portico and some

newly-painted Tudor was a cream stucco-fronted shop which I
took for a pub from the exquisite windmill sign. This turned out
to be an advertisement for a particular make of bread, and the shop
a baker's. From this corner a covered alley leaves the square,
making a perfect frame for a diminutive gem of black and white
timbering, which faces warm mellowed brick across a cobbled
lane. Twice I went back into the entry to savour the picture. The
steeple rises in the middle of the north side of the square from
behind a red pantiled roof with three dormer windows. As I
looked back from TEES' deck before going below for the night into
the snug three-berthed cabin, some alchemy of the town's lighting
had turned the night sky to a delicate violet behind a ghostly spire.
I could happily live in Newark.

"It's a quarter past six and I've got some water boiling if you
want a mash." Thus the British Waterways watchman as he
roused us on Monday. I had slept like a log in the skipper's bunk,
but he was aboard in time to sample our mash after a very early
start from Nottingham. We were off before 7 a.m. with 74 miles
between us and Hull, mists swirled from the water and drifted
thick above, but opened at times into reassuring windows of
delicate blue with a hint of gold where the sun shone on the upper
layers. Jackdaws were astir on the castle walls. We puffed beneath
Newark's Trent Bridge, past an agricultural implement works,
alongside the Trent Concrete & Gravel Wharf, left behind us
more maltings, and negotiated the tricky turn under the
Nottingham – Lincoln Railway. Usually it is necessary to
unhook the tow to do this, but our barges had gone ahead and tied
up for the night at the tail of the Nether Lock, where we roped up
again and left the cut for the Trent which came in on our left.
While we worked the sluices of Nether Lock, a man in overalls
fished an oar from among a heap of stop planks and, sculling over
the stern, guided a small coble into the entrance of a large gravel
pit to his day's work.

A straight reach on the Trent is known as a 'rack' or 'yowster',
and as we glided down Winthorpe Rack the sun and the mist
fought for mastery in a welter of gold. By the time we were in
'The Ovens' the morning had resolved itself into a glory of green,

blue, and silver, alive with herons, wagtails, martins, and magpies. We were heading for less-wooded country than yesterday, but still small assemblies of trees lined the banks, and at a group of elms known as 'The Crow Trees' there was an inscribed plate commemorating the old boatman whose ashes had been scattered at his request on the river. Doubtless he had known and loved such beauty as we saw at Cromwell Lock — which is worthy a less repulsive name. Behind the lock-house an ash grove hung its yellowing seeds to match the feathery clumps of tansy below. Beside the lock the weir threshed up such an expanse of detergent foam that to look down on it from the lock wall, dazzling white in the now triumphant sun, was like looking down on a sea of cotton-wool cloud from an aircraft.

We locked down with STANTON, a motor-barge full of yellow stone for bank repairs, the four of us finding ample space in the lock. There is a large sill to be crossed out of the bottom gate, and an additional gate of a flood lock is often used to raise the water level sufficiently to do this. We were confident of crossing the sill in our unloaded state, but STANTON was lower in the water. She scraped her bottom, but with our weight alongside and the two barges behind, and by picking her coble from aft and slinging it for'ard with the crane on her deck to raise her stern, she was shoved into deeper water which, Cromwell Lock being the last in the river, was now tidal. It is high tide at Cromwell six hours later than Hull.

Locks usually provide their bit of banter and this was no exception. One of the helpers on the lock wall removed his cap to mop his brow after a spell on the sluice wheels and revealed an entirely bald pate. "Lovely head of skin you've got there" bawled the skipper.

The tail of Cromwell Lock marks the site of a Roman bridge, some of which was removed from the river bed in 1884, and a small stone on the bank records this fact. STANTON went ahead of us where the Legions once crossed, and demonstrated the force with which the water raced from the weir as she was pushed almost broadside with foam suds ballooning over her.

From now on the tide was our preoccupation. At Sutton-on-

Trent, where Nobby assured me they still have a 'tupping-post' on which the locals bash their heads for sport, we had no wish to emulate them by ramming our head aground. The huge bend here is one of the places where a good depth of water is essential. Red beaches shelve into the stream from low clear-cut banks, and submerged shoals await the unwary helmsman. The spot is called the 'Milking Boat' — I could not discover why — and glad we were when it was safely passed and the grey-white tower of Sutton receded astern. But one hazard overcome, another confronted us in the 80 yards of Normanton Dyke, a narrow island in midstream with one willow and a tangle of mugwort, ragwort and thistles.

"A horrible place to pass," said Nobby, and the words were hardly uttered when TEES' sister-ship THAMES approached us, followed by another boat. Again all went well, and we persevered downstream between scenes of pleasing monotony, cattle on the field skyline or knee deep in water, herd upon herd of that exellent milker, the Lincoln Red Shorthorn. We were now well among the flat lands of the eastern counties, and Fledborough Bridge reminded me of the Kiel Canal bridges with its long causeways on either side of the river to return its rail track gradually to ground level. Trent is prolific in local names for river features — 'Hully-Gully', 'Hooton's Nose', 'Scotchman's Shoal', 'Moses' Mouth', 'Juggler's Holt', 'Blotah Dyke', 'Misbegotten Shoal', and 'No Man's Friend' among them. 'Sweetapple's Dyke' near Fledborough is named after the Rev. William Sweetapple, Rector of Fledborough from 1712 to 1755, who ran his own private Gretna Green, supplying licence and marriage lines on the same day regardless of the couple's domicile. In 1755 Parliament stopped this matrimonial racket, and in the same year Mr. Sweetapple died.

It was a 26-foot tide at Hull, and we were now meeting it, and with it several gravel boats of the Lincoln & Hull Water Transport Company which left Hull on the tide around 3 a.m. The river was now the county boundary between Nottinghamshire and Lincoln, and on the Lincoln or starboard side (the term is permissible in tidal waters) on an enormous loop called Dunham Dubs, beneath a red hill, the bank had been lowered and a flood bank raised 100 yards back from the river. At Torksey the Trent is joined from the east by Foss Dyke. Excavated around 120 A.D. by the Romans, it was intended primarily for drainage, but may have been used for navigation. In any case it is the oldest artificial navigation in Britain. James I offered three baronetcies to the city of Lincoln for sale to raise money for work on the Foss Dyke. For all its many vicissitudes, Foss Dyke is still navigable to Lincoln 15 miles away, dead straight but for one bend, and Nobby had been along it with cargoes of fertilizer, flour, wheat, and newsprint on other boats. Had the tide been higher we should have been able to see Lincoln Cathedral, for the morning was becoming exceptionally clear, but we were not high enough up the river banks for this remarkable long view. Leaving the junction, we passed Torksey Castle downstream, merely a bizarre wall of red brick on a grey base in a meadow. The grey tower of a church, a railway bridge with one arch on an island, and we were beyond Torksey.

The morning was settling down pleasantly as we chugged through 'the Potteries', chillier than yesterday, the cloud less placid, being mist from the North Sea piled up on an east wind, but rising and dispersing nicely. The broad river, agitated slightly by the incoming tide, mirrored the sky; chocolate-coloured bullocks came down to the water on the low green banks, and I might well have been on my beloved Lower Lough Erne in County Fermanagh but the tower which rose before me was the old windmill of Marton, not the faery round tower on Devenish Island. Breaking in on my memories of that loveliest of lands, Ireland, one sylvan scene, rather out of character on the lower Trent, was Knaith Hall, its black and white embowered in trees beside a hillocky stretch of bank.

By Gainsborough's three-arched bridge dated 1791, which we reached at noon, the day had become one to remember for a lifetime. Light, flooding in from every angle, had chased away nearly all the cloud, leaving just sufficient to give distinction to the vast inverted bowl of sky. This was beauty beyond description — frankness, clarity, limpidity. Constable would have been enraptured as I was, and his brush would have conveyed much more than my pen.

George Eliot, a novelist from my native Warwickshire, chose Trent as her Floss, and Gainsborough as the St. Ogg's of *The Mill on the Floss*. 'On this mighty tide,' she wrote, 'the black ships — laden with the fresh-scented fir-planks, with rounded sacks of oil-bearing seed, or with the dark glitter of coal — are borne along to the town of St. Ogg's, which shows its aged, fluted red roofs and the broad gables of the wharves. . . . ' I find George Eliot's novels unreadable, but commend her as one of the few who have chosen the canal as a theme for poetry:

> 'Our brown canal was endless to my thought;
> And on its banks I sat in dreamy peace,
> Unknowing how the good I loved was wrought,
> Untroubled by the fear that it would cease.
> Slowly the barges floated into view
> Rounding a grassy hill to me sublime
> With some Unknown beyond it, whither flew
> The parting cuckoo toward a fresh spring time.
> The wide-arched bridge, the scented elder flowers,
> The wondrous watery rings that died too soon,
> The echoes of the quarry, the still hours
> With white robe sweeping on the shadeless noon,
> Were but my growing self, are part of me,
> My present Past, my root of piety.'

The canal where George Eliot mused must have been the Coventry Canal near the junction with the Ashby-de-la-Zouch branch.

In 1815 Gainsborough saw the first steam-packet in Lincolnshire waters, the CALEDONIA, built in Glasgow and brought round via the Caledonian Canal to ply between Gainsborough and Hull as a cargo and passenger boat. The Trent is busy enough today at Gainsborough, from Spiller's jetty to the new silo on the northern end of the waterfront. Craft of the Hull & Fossdyke Lighterage Company were unloading timber; bags of cattle meal were being transferred by crane from the holds of a barge to the British Oil and Cake Mills. Boats were disgorging wheat in three different ways — by suction pipe, elevator scoop, and in bags by crane. One motor barge was full of metal turnings which it would dump in the river downstream. At the northern edge of the town, where a ship-building yard was spilled over to the west bank, the mate tootled loudly on our hooter and was rewarded by handkerchiefs waving from a distant bedroom window at the home of some relatives. Gainsborough's last outpost was a stark red building, solitary on the river bank, said to be the original of Dorlcote Mill in George Eliot's book. Nearby, a great breach occurred in the eastern bank some six years ago and 30 square miles of countryside were flooded. At Gainsborough, 42 miles from Hull, TEES' crew have seen a seal and a porpoise.

The Stockwiths, East and West, had their Ferry House Inn, and, on the Nottinghamshire bank, the entrance lock to the Chesterfield Canal, a British Waterways warehouse beside it. Downstream of the Stockwiths, Lincolnshire jumps the river to take in the Isle of Axholme, and the Trent remains entirely in Lincolnshire for the rest of its course to the Humber.

Industry now reared its head again. The three chimneys of Keadby Power Station were duplicated in the calm water before us, while many miles to northward the Frodingham Iron & Steel Company's gehenna monopolised the horizon and sent its murk skyward, giving a coppery tint to the pellucid blue. By 'ness' and 'bight' we carried steadily on, tacking to and fro to keep the channel though the river was over 100 yards wide. These terms are used on bends, the 'bight' being the broad sweep of the outside, while the 'ness' is the nose or shelf of sand on the inside of the curve. Our landmarks were Butterwick Church, where TEES always checks the time by the clock; an old tower mill converted into a residence; and Keadby Bridge which carried the railway between Grimsby and Doncaster. The navigation arch of this bridge opens because it was made to pass the masts of Humber 'sloops' and 'keels'. The coping stones of one of its buttresses are a valuable aid to navigation. If six of them are completely above water level on the ebb, TEES is in no danger of grounding in the Humber. If nine are showing, grounding is so certain that it waits for the tide to turn. With eight and a bit visible we were threatened with a sporting passage, and Nobby hurried to let water out of the stern ballast tanks.

We saw our first sea-going merchant ships at Keadby, the 800-ton coasters SEDULITY and SUMMITY from London. They were taking on board coal brought to the river from Doncaster, Denaby, or Brighouse by the Sheffield & South Yorkshire Navigation which has its junction upstream of them. Just north of Keadby we felt the first ominous scraping on the bottom, while overhead the glorious day was blighted and defiled by fumes and smoke from the Frodingham works, and grit made our eyes smart. Off Flixborough Stather the GALLIUM of Caen was discharging iron ore into rail wagons for the steel works. We scraped our way seaward beneath the artificial cloud, with TEES stopping once completely, only to jerk forward as the barges bumped her stern.

As the sun asserted itself again we could see the gentle line of the Yorkshire Wolds, quilt-patterned on the far side of the Humber. To the east a high wooded ridge was accompanying the Trent, to fall into the river at Cliff End, a scrubby hillside just before the confluence with the Humber. Black-backed gulls were strutting on the sandbanks around us. This was nearly the estuary. Bump, scrape, bounce, pitch: TEES grounding and being 'stemmed' by the barges. The river was 300 yards wide, but our great test lay just ahead where two sand-bars closed in from either bank, the cows on each almost merging in one group. More scraping and more bumping. The river narrowed to 100 yards. But we did it, to cruise triumphantly past the first light beacon into the broad Humber. At a red-painted light tower we turned to starboard into a bounding breeze from the North Sea. We had outwitted Trent Falls at dead low water, and as the tide began to flow, in muddy brown wavelets, an occasional playful splash was flung aboard. Another 16½ miles to Hull.

But we were not out of the wood — or the mud — yet. Did not Lord Noel Buxton walk across the Humber only a week earlier at Whitton to prove the existence of a Roman ford? And had I not, on a salmon story in the spring, seen the lave-net fishermen walk right across just such another estuary on the Severn, at Awre, nearly two miles to New Grounds on the opposite shore? For a while TEES hugged the south shore of the Humber, and then plunged boldly across towards Yorkshire. The mate was plying the sounding rod which showed six feet of water beneath us — sometimes less. The north shore safely attained, we skirted a mudbank past Upper and Middle Whitton lightships, and then, off Brough aerodrome, turned for the Lincolnshire coast again to outflank a tawny sandbank lying athwart the estuary. This course brought us up to Lower Whitton lightship off Read's Island, a flat pasture rising from the mud, haunt of lapwings which took off with erratic flight at our close approach. We watched the last moments of a white butterfly which lighted momentarily on the water, took off, dropped again, and was overwhelmed by the tiniest of white horses. To starboard, behind the seaward end of Read's Island, the Ancholme entered the Humber at Ferriby Sluice. This canalised river is navigable to the Lincolnshire town of Brigg with its sugar factory, and for 10 miles further south.

The boats which had left Hull on the afternoon tide were now ploughing upstream towards us, low in the water, a colourful flotilla. Petroleum boats and motor barges they were, dumb barges under tow, puffing tugs green with yellow lines; orange, white, and black hulls; pale blue white and pink; yellow-nosed; red and deep blue; two short lilac barges, the type that ply the Aire & Calder Navigation via Goole for Leeds, Wakefield, and other industrial towns of the West Riding. Again we changed course and made for Hessle, leaving Barton-on-Humber behind us. I saw, as I did on the Severn, the amazing powers of identification of these boatmen. Nobby pointed out DEE, a sister-ship of TEES, towing one dumb barge; the coaster WATERSMEET bound for Keadby; and other distant boats familiar to him. And the mate blew a fanfare on the hooter to greet his father, skipper of Harker's BANNERDALE H, bound upstream half-a-mile away.

Visually and otherwise the Hull Fish Dock had now impressed itself on our notice to the exclusion of all else. We cruised beside its long wall with fish-curing plants and icing plants, for all the world like the back end of a Midlands factory on the cut. Water gushed from countless overflows and a foul stink pervaded the river despite the cold breeze. Making our way past a couple of

German timber boats, we cast off our tow and chugged into the Old Harbour, to tie up third boat out from the quayside with our barges dropping in beside us. Before, behind, and across the harbour were innumerable boats — tugs, barges, coasters. We were almost landlocked by boats.

So I came again to Kingston-upon-Hull. It was just such a lovely September day when I first saw Hull in 1929, as I sailed from Victoria Dock for Finland. I was a boy of 18 faced with my first serious adventure in travel. Friends used to ask, as I followed my Finland trip with others to outlandish places like Iceland, Spitzbergen, Poland, and the Balearic Islands, why I did not see my own country first. My answer was that it was more likely some future job would enable me to see Britain than to travel farther afield, and that, in any case, I could see my own islands when the urge for foreign travel had died. Little did I imagine then that I should have a job which would take me from Shetland to Scilly, from Yarmouth to Dublin. Even less did I realise, as I do now, that there is more satisfaction in knowing the local canal thoroughly than in superficial visits to foreign countries. And of all the means whereby I have seen England, none is more rewarding, and none gets so close to the heart of things as travel by canal and river with the men who know those waterways thoroughly.

It was six o'clock when we tied up, so I washed and wandered into 'old Hull'. The Old Harbour was the haven for whalers in bygone days. Beside it, Wilberforce House, home of the man who killed the slave trade, has been restored, its green lawns in remarkable contrast to its surroundings. I found my way to that most romantic-named of all streets, The Land of Green Ginger, and dawdled about the cobbled alleys of the dock-side, like Bishop Lane Staithe, with offices buried in their dingy depths, offices where, I felt, great mercantile enterprises may have sprung. But Hull is a thriving modern municipality. Among other things it owns its telephone service which costs a penny less than Post Office telephones for a local call.

John Turnbull, my photgraphic colleague, arrived at night to take me back to Birmingham by car, collecting pictures of the

Trent and the canals en route. As both Nobby and Bob had gone to their homes to sleep, there were bunks for John and me aboard TEES. Twice during the night I was awakened by something like the Crack of Doom; once when TEES and a few dozen other boats settled on the mud as the tide ran out, and again when we all lifted on the incoming waters. My ultimate awaking was not unlike the previous morning. This time it was Jim off one of our barges, and he went one better than the Newark watchman, actually making our mash and serving a cup each in bed. Engineer and mate were aboard by 7 a.m. and soon we were out on a misty Humber, its oily stream burnished copper by a blood-red sun, dropping the barges at Victoria Dock for barley, and continuing to Alexandra Dock ourselves for crating timber which would go on by road from Nottingham to Birmingham for packing Hercules bicycles. The timber was aboard KETTY DANIELSEN, a Dane, and as the hatches were being opened we took our farewell of TEES' crew and drove south.

We took photographs at Gainsborough, Torksey, and Newark. At the Torksey entrance lock to Foss Dyke the lockside is strikingly similar to a country railway station, with the blue and yellow of British Waterways plastered liberally on lamp brackets, railings, buildings, and on the capstans for opening the lock gates — a new feature to me. Then from Nottingham I worked out an itinerary which would enable me to see all I had missed on Saturday. I felt it was cheating to do the middle section of the Birmingham – Hull route at the end, in reverse direction and by car, but as it turned out I should have seen little more on foot, and the prospect of a lift by boat seemed unlikely.

Trent Lock can fairly be considered the junction of the Trent & Mersey Canal with the River Trent although an artificial cut continues for nearly another mile to circumvent the weir downstream of the confluence of the Soar and Trent. I know of no better 'plum' for the waterways connoisseur, for the community at Trent Lock has grown up solely to serve the boatmen, though now they are almost entirely pleasure-seekers, and their too palatial boathouse with green lawns and many sailing boats strikes the one alien note in a quaint backwater. It is the junction of three counties, Nottinghamshire, Derby, and Leicestershire, and of four waterways. We drove from Sawley well over a mile down a road which came to an end at the Navigation Inn, white-fronted and attractive beside a chestnut tree. Facing it across the verdant surface of the Erewash Canal was the even more comely Erewash Navigation Inn, white-fronted also with green window frames and shaded by a clean-limbed beech. Beside this second inn is the lock-keeper's house, and British Waterways have a new warehouse there dated 1950.

The Trent, having last merged with the Trent & Mersey Canal at Sawley Cut nearly a mile upstream, flows broad and beautiful past Trent Lock, veering to the right to be joined 400 yards downstream beneath a wooded ridge by the River Soar. This canalised river, part of the Grand Union system, comes up from the main Birmingham – London line at Long Buckby through Leicester and Loughborough. Houseboats lined the Erewash Canal, its green surface stretching like close-cropped lawns before them. Very little moves on the Erewash today, though I did hear of a pair of boats which take slack to Long Eaton factories occasionally. The same informant, who dispenses ice-cream in a tea-room beside the Navigation Inn, told me that before the war the two pubs were populous each night with Fellows, Morton, & Clayton boatmen, many from Birmingham. During the war the Trent & Mersey had its last fling when supplies for the U.S. Forces in the east of England were brought from Liverpool by canal.

The old village of Sawley, through which we drove after leaving Trent Lock, grew as a canal village, and the inhabitants are still known locally as 'Sawley nose-bags' because so many of them used to set out to work on the canal daily with the horse's food slung over their shoulders. At Shardlow I learned another local name, a canal basin being referred to as a 'nick'. And yet another, 'ridge' instead of 'channel' for the deep navigable part of the cut. There is some pleasing canal architecture in the warehouse at Shardlow, and a graceful arch where a 'nick' runs under the Trent Corn Mills of F.E. Stevens Ltd. The same firm now uses as a corn drier what was once a soap factory with its own 'nick'. Somewhere between soap and corn the building had been a miniature rifle range.

Shardlow was an honoured name in the heyday of canals, but a young man in a garage beside the overgrown cut said it was a month since last he saw a cargo boat pass.

We played hide-and-seek with the reedy course of the canal past Aston-upon-Trent and Weston-upon-Trent, and at Swarkeston found its crystal waters overhung with enormous coltsfoot leaves and given over to fishermen. Crossing to the south of the canal we continued 'twixt it and Trent to Willington, canal and river running on parallel courses, never much more than a mile apart, and often nearly touching. The river bridge at Swarkeston was built by two ladies whose lovers were reputed to have drowned while ferrying across to visit them. Canal travel had made me very church-tower conscious, but of all the attractive architecture I had seen from canals nothing was more lovely than the slender finger of Repton spire, seen to advantage from the canal near Swarkeston.

The Trent & Mersey was the brainchild of the great Brindley, that almost illiterate engineering genius. It was to constitute the north-western and north-eastern arms of 'The Cross' which would unite England's four main estuaries, Mersey, Humber, Thames, and Severn, in silver links of water. Because of its importance in his scheme, Brindley wanted the canal to be known as the Grand Trunk, and that name has been interchangeable with Trent & Mersey throughout its history. The Act of Parliament was obtained in 1766, in which year Josiah Wedgwood cut the first turf at Bramhills. Brindley had undertaken to complete the canal in five years, but on September 27th, 1772, when six years had already elapsed, he died at the age of 56 of a chill contracted while surveying the Caldon branch of the canal. It was another five years before the Grand Trunk was finished.

A typical Brindley feature on the eastern horn of the canal is the aqueduct on which it crosses the River Dove near Burton — a bed of earth and puddled clay in a casing of brick, so different from the cast iron troughs in which Telford was to carry his canals over roads and rivers. Within 300 yards of the aqueduct two other bridges span the Dove: one a graceful ancient stone bridge which carried the old Derby road, the other carrying the modern highway which approaches the river across its water meadows already on stilts.

Horninglow Wharf, Burton, where — if anywhere — I expected to see signs of life on the Grand Trunk, was given up to its new inheritors, four cabin cruisers. An agitated moorhen clucked to its young in the iris rushes in the shadow of the busy Tutbury road bridge. This bridge, and a warehouse astride the canal, make a small tunnel where fishes played in the clear water. The doors which opened on to boats in the gloom are long since bolted and barred, and an old crane stands, the last solitary guardian of the past.

I stopped at Alrewas to see where the Trent passes through the canal, entering it from the north at the tail of a lock, flowing in the same channel for 200 yards, and leaving the south bank by a weir. Alrewas showed pleasing signs of potential use of the canal in the boats of Mallabar & Prince, civil engineers and contractors, moored between the bridge and the lock. There were two iron butties, BUNNY and JENNY, and a motor PRINCE CHARLES, registered at Kidderminster, of all places. And here, almost at the end of a series of journeys which began two years earlier on NORMAN CHAMBERLAIN, I had a pleasant and coincidental encounter. Tied up below the bridge was a converted butty without a name. I was invited aboard by her owner, Mr Wallis who, with his wife, lives on the butty in the Erewash Canal at Trent Lock. NORMAN CHAMBERLAIN entered the conversation, which led Mr Wallis to tell me that he bought his butty, three years before, at the same yard — Element's of Oldbury — where NORMAN CHAMBERLAIN, then RUBY, was bought for the Birmingham Federation of Boys' Clubs. His boat had been THELMA, but before that she was CAPTAIN CUTTLE, named after the Derby winner in the year she was built, 1922. Mr Wallis calls her CAPTAIN CUTTLE, and one day hopes to get round to painting the name on her bends. A leisurely life, canal life!

Mr Wallis had done much bow-hauling from the Erewash to Alrewas. He told me that the locks east of Stenson are double. Alrewas Lock was single with single top and double bottom gates, dated 1921, the balance beams recently painted in cream and dove-grey squares. It was four months since Mr Wallis had seen working boats on the Grand Trunk — a pair with powdered milk from Liverpool for Nottingham, and a steerer who swore he would never plough this particular furrow again.

My last call was at Fradley Junction. I left the car to walk the last hundred or more yards along the canal to the junction. To westward a brilliant sun which had drenched the earth with golden warmth all day became even more dazzling as it sank lower. No hedge or other impediment divided the canal from the narrow road which I trod. Nestling in the reeds on the far bank were several narrow boats, British Waterways SNIPE among them, its name-bird depicted on the cabin wall. Beyond them was a field like a thousand others I had seen from England's canals. Ahead was a bridge, replica of a thousand at which I had hazarded my cranium — and a bridge-hole where the motor's chugging engine breaks into an exultant shout within the confines of the echoing brick.

A railing faces the actual junction at Fradley with a seat attached where generations of boatmen have supped their pints at 'The Swan' on just such lovely evenings, while pale blue smoke rising from their butty chimneys has told of a meal in preparation. What talk there must have been of happenings at places unknown off the world of the cut — Napton, Norbury, Autherley, Huddlesford, Foxton, Audlem, Tardebigge, 'Maffers', Cowroast — the junctions and the locks, each a metropolis on the once busy network of waterways. Those days, one fears, are gone. But the canals are not yet dead. There is a revival of interest in those who cruise the landlocked waterways for pleasure. Recreation may yet save what industry cannot.

This route from Birmingham to Hull, for instance, is still practicable, and the regular passage of a boat or two works wonders in keeping down the weeds. The Coventry Canal stretched its silver length southward from where I sat musing, to disappear beneath a red swing bridge into the green shade of Fradley Wood. Two hundred yards west of the junction the last lock fell from the Mersey, while nearer at hand in the opposite direction the first dropped down towards the Trent. The warm red brick of 'The Swan' and the adjacent warehouse, the yellowing sycamore before the dilapidated slate-tiled toll house across the water, two tree-bordered houses, contented hens in a wire enclosure, all slumbered in the sun. What had been a busy junction in a more leisurely, gracious world, was dead, but for an overloaded hay-wagon rumbling slowly down a road from the sunset.

So much for Brindley's dream, his Grand Trunk. Roaring above, contemptuous of the earth below, an aircraft took off from behind Fradley Wood. Much progress of benefit to mankind has been made, but I am convinced with William Scawen Blount that, in matters of transport at least:

> 'The new world still is all less fair
> Than the old world it mocks.'

Then I realised that the nearby R.A.F. Station from which the noisy juggernauts erupted into the skies is a School of Navigation. So the old name is retained after all, though its young devotees, as smart in their blue uniforms as the young officer crossing the bridge on a motor-bike, would find it a shocking bind to be referred to as 'navvies', as were the men who constructed the 'canal navigations' when they were the last word in transport 200 years ago.

Index

Dunstall Park Racecourse 145.

Eagle & Sun (Hanbury) 80.
Eakring 181.
Earlswood 90, 92.
Eccleshall Road Bridge 153.
Edgbaston 29.
Edwards, John 87, 92, 105.
Elements (carriers) 33, 168–69, 196.
Ellesmere & Chester Canal 147.
Ellesmere Port 10, 23, 32, 34, 132,
 147, 150, 159, 162–63.
Elliott's Metal Co. 29.
Emscote 109.
English & Welsh Grounds Lightship
 56.
Enoch's Wharf, Hockley Heath 88,
 104.
Erewash Canal 106, 196.
Erewash Navigation Inn 194.
ERNEST THOMAS 103.
Ettingshall Junior School 47.

Factory Locks 36, 40.
Farmer's Locks 10, 23.
Fazeley 130, 165–66, 168, 170.
Featherbed Lane Bridge 97.
Fellows, Morton & Clayton Ltd 21,
 81, 128, 165–66, 194.
Fenny Stratford 119–21.
Fenton, Ernie 43, 45.
Ferriby Sluice 191.
Fir Tree Inn, Oddingley 80.
Flatholm 56.
Fledborough Bridge 186.
Fleur-de-Lys Hotel 94.
Flint, Bob 16, 18, 20, 116.
Flixborough 190.
FLOWER OF GLOSTER 85, 95.
FLYING ENTERPRISE 53.
Forest of Dean 64.
FORGET-ME-NOT 129.
Foss Dyke 175, 187, 193.
Foxton 197.
Fradley 10, 170–71, 197–98.
Framilode 74.
Frampton 73–4.
Freeman, Walter 93.

Frodingham Iron & Steel Co.
 189–90.

Gainsborough 179–80, 187–89,
 193.
GAINSBOROUGH and SAVERTON 110.
GALLIUM 190.
Gas Street Basin 10, 30, 79, 92.
Gawn Housing Estate 39.
Gayton 116.
George Griffiths boats 33.
GILMAN KEVEN 80–1.
Gnosall 152–3.
Glascote 165.
Gloucester 58–9, 63, 73–76, 78.
Gloucester & Berkeley Canal 10, 29,
 54, 63.
Goodwin, George 11.
Goole 177, 191.
Gorsty Hill Tunnel 26, 38–40.
Grand Canal, Ireland 79.
Grand Junction Canal 106.
Grand Trunk Canal (Trent &
 Mersey) 195–98.
Grand Union Canal 10, 32, 80, 84,
 101–2, 105–6, 111, 113, 115,
 121, 123–24, 129–30, 166–68,
 194.
Great Linford 120.
Great Western Railway 9, 73n, 85,
 91, 93, 99.
Greenfield Lock 160.
Grimsby 177, 189.
Guest, Ken 103, 106, 113, 119, 125.
Gunthorpe Bridge 179.
Gunthorpe Weir 180.
Guttridge, Mrs 43.

Halesowen 30, 37, 39, 46.
Hall, Mrs Ellen 44.
HALVARD BRATT 55.
Hamstead Colliery 46.
Hanslope 119.
Happy Valley 91.
Hardwick Bridge 97.
Harker, John & Co. Ltd 58–9, 191.
Harrow 129.
Hartley Arms, Wheaton Aston 151.

LEITRIM 64.
LEO (tug) 128.
Lickey Hills 20.
Lickey Incline 18.
Limehouse 106.
Lincoln 128, 184, 186–87.
Lincoln & Hull Water Transport
  Co. 186.
Little Gaddesden 123.
Liverpool 30, 147, 194, 197.
Llangollen Canal 157, 160.
Llanthony Bridge 75.
London 14, 21, 84, 101, 105, 121,
  125, 129, 135, 167–68, 172, 194.
London & North Western Railway
  119, 147.
Long Buckby 110, 115, 194.
Long Eaton 194.
Long Itchington 111.
Lower Avon Navigation Trust 100,
  128.
Lower Lode, Tewkesbury 77.
Lower Lough Erne 187.
Loughborough & Leicester
  Navigation 106.
Loughborough 194.
Lowsonford 92, 94.
LOYAL BRITON 56.
Lydney 62.
LYNX 81.

Maisemore Arm 76.
Malin, Ken 16.
MALLABAR and PRINCE 196.
Manchester Ship Canal 10, 21, 34,
  132, 134, 147, 163–64.
MARGARET HAM 56.
Market Drayton 154–55.
Market Harborough 106, 110.
Marsworth ('Maffers') 123–24, 166,
  197.
Marton 187.
Mary Arden's House 97.
Matthewman, Win 27, 40, 42–3.
May, Jim 57–8.
Meadow Lane, Nottingham
  174–75, 177.
Medway Oil Storage Co. 181.

Merrell, Dennis 79.
Mersey, River 10–11, 147, 163,
  195, 197.
Middlewich Branch Canal 155, 157.
Midland Tar Distillers Ltd 20, 32.
'Milking Boat' 186.
Ministry of Transport Women's
  Training Scheme 101, 130.
Minworth 130, 168–69.
Mond's Gas Works 40.
Monk Meadow 74.
Monmore Green Wharf 45–6.
Monmouth 51.
Montgomeryshire Canal 147.
Moore, Fred 31–2, 49.
Moreton-in-Marsh to Shipston-on-
  Stour Tramway 99.
Morgan, Skipper Leslie 57.
Mould, Jack 16.
MR LINTHORST HOMAN 56.
Mullett family 46.

NANCY and NELSON 110.
Nantwich 148, 154–55, 157.
Napton 112–13, 197.
Nash Court, Shropshire 82.
Nash Mills 126.
Navigation Inn, Erewash 194.
Navigation Inn, Gnosall 152.
Navigation Inn, Wootton Wawen
  96.
Nechells Gas Works 9, 20, 22, 24.
Nelson, George 109.
Nene, River 106.
NEPTUNE and MARY 119.
Nestles Factory 128.
Nether Lock 179, 184.
Netherton Tunnel 26, 36–7, 40, 46,
  135.
Netherwood Farm, Oddingley
  79–80.
Newark 128, 175, 177–78, 181–84,
  193.
New Bradwell 119.
Newport (Shropshire) and Canal
  152–53.
Newport Pagnell 120.